T0036660

Arnold Hollinger, 1955
La Habana Vieja

Text and photos by Heidi Hollinger
Project Editor: Agnès Saint-Laurent
Art Direction & Design: Josée Amyotte
Revision: Alison Ramsey
Proofreading: Robert Ronald
Other photos by:
Rondo Banks: C2, Top Picks Reason #86, pages 8 and
    241, Reasons #112, 124, 125, 141, 212, 238, 252,
    253, 280;
Nathali Soave: C4, Top Picks Reason #17, Reason #63;
Casey Stoll: Reason #125;
Osmel Azcuy: Reason #300.

Reason #247 A part of the text was already
published in an article by Heidi Hollinger for the
magazine *ExtraBrut*.

Bibliothèque et Archives nationales du Québec and
Library and Archives Canada Cataloguing in
Publication

Title: 300 reasons to love Havana / Heidi Hollinger.
Other titles: Three hundred reasons to love Havana
Names: Hollinger, Heidi, author.
Description: 2nd edition.
Identifiers: Canadiana (print) 20230071104 |
Canadiana (ebook) 20230071112 | ISBN
9781988002989 | ISBN 9781988002996 (eBook)
Subjects: LCSH: Havana (Cuba)—Guidebooks. |
LCGFT: Guidebooks.
Classification: LCC F1799.H33 H64 2024 | DDC
917.291/23047—dc23

Marie-Joëlle Parent
Creator of the "300 Reasons to Love" collection
Author of *300 Reasons to Love New York*
and *300 Reasons to Love San Francisco*

EXCLUSIVE DISTRIBUTOR:

For Canada and the United States:
Simon & Schuster Canada
166 King Street East, Suite 300
Toronto, ON M5A 1J3
phone: (647) 427-8882
    1-800-387-0446
Fax: (647) 430-9446
simonandschuster.ca

NOTE TO THE READERS
All preconceptions have to be abandoned. If you
try to judge Havana by familiar paradigms, you are
heading for a misunderstanding! To the best of my
ability, everything is accurate at the time of press.

01-24

© 2024, 2018 Juniper Publishing,
division of the Sogides Group Inc.,
a subsidiary of Québecor Média Inc.
(Montreal, Quebec)

Printed in Canada
All rights reserved

Legal deposit: 2024
National Library of Québec
National Library of Canada

ISBN (paper) 978-2-1988002-98-9
ISBN (digital) 978-2-1988002-99-6

Conseil des arts   Canada Council
du Canada   for the Arts

We gratefully acknowledge the support of the Canada
Council for the Arts for its publishing program.

We acknowledge the financial support of the
Government of Canada through the Canada Book Fund
for our publishing activities.

HEIDI HOLLINGER

300

REASONS TO LOVE
HAVANA

In Honour of Eusebio Leal

Contents

Preface

I t is a great pleasure to present 300 Reasons to Love Havana, the fifth in a series that I began with *300 Reasons to Love New York*.

After New York, San Francisco, Paris and Montreal, I am thrilled to be adding Havana to this series of guidebooks.

I can't think of a better person than Heidi Hollinger to reveal to us the hidden treasures of the Cuban capital as it opens to the world!

I've had great admiration for Heidi from the moment I discovered her portraits of politicians in her book The Russians Emerge, over 10 years ago now. I have interviewed her several times over my career as a journalist, and have always been fascinated by the paths she has pursued and her bold approach to life.

She spent 10 years in Russia during the early glory days of the post-Soviet era. She had access to the highest political circles in the country. She revolutionized the world of photography with her "non-iconic" images of political leaders. She rubbed shoulders with Vladimir Putin, the Dalai Lama and Fidel Castro. She has exhibited her work in major galleries in Moscow and as far afield as Siberia.

I started this series because I wanted travelers to have insider access to the best places to go, and to be introduced to the lively personalities that animate a city and make it unique. And this is exactly what you'll find in Heidi's book, even if you've been to Cuba several times before.

In it, Heidi shares her favorite spots, some of which she's been going to for more than 30 years. She introduces us to emerging artists. She takes us out of Old Havana on an electric bike ride to a jungle in the middle of the city, or to a small fishing village that has become a paradise of mosaics.

Heidi fell in love with Havana on a trip she took in 1989, while studying modern languages at McGill University. The charmingly anachronistic city became a second home to her. She even found another family there, including Selene, her "Cuban grandma," from whom she rented a room for 25 years. She is one of the inspirations for this book.

Above all, it was the people of Havana that captivated Heidi from her very first visit there. Their warm smiles, authenticity, resourcefulness and resilience have left an indelible mark on her, and this comes through clearly in her book. Heidi is an inquisitive traveler who is able to make connections with people, who in turn respond candidly to her lens. Her portraits of the city's inhabitants will remain etched in my memory forever. This book is truly a love letter to Havana.

Marie-Joëlle Parent

Creator of the "300 Reasons to Love" collection

Author of *300 Reasons to Love New York* and *300 Reasons to Love San Francisco*.

Havana Blues

For Heidi Hollinger, a true citizen of the world...

From time to time, a petite, attractive woman—camera in hand—roams the streets of Havana. She first came here more than 20 years ago as a tourist, and over time has evolved into a true *habanera*. It was a love affair with the city with always something new to find, discover or uncover.

Heidi, you are always covered by the colors of Havana, the secrets of the lights: soft when dawn breaks, and intense as the sun sets. Blue is the color of nostalgia at every corner, on every street—that's what makes this place different for you... Heidi, it's a soft voice calling you back time and again.

It is difficult to describe a city in a few words. Havana has recently become a destination for travelers from around the world. But that wasn't always the case. The city, once isolated behind a wall of political "misinformation" was, and still is, just 90 miles from the U.S. coast, and yet it was out of reach for the majority to the north.

The forbidden-city status made Havana an alluring place for many. Now they arrive by the thousands, trying to put their finger on the attraction that lures them like a magnet. I came to Havana from New York City when I was 18 to see what it was all about. Photography was my excuse, but as time when by, I slowly but surely became a *habanero* falling in love with something that I could not describe.

For me, Havana is all about color—and mood, like New Orleans Blues. Blue is nostalgia, blue is the start of another day, blue is the water that splashes against the walls of the Malecón. Havana is yesterday stopped in time, in old buildings and homes along narrow cobblestone streets, with vendors from a bygone era, and the waft of morning coffee.

Havana carries you back in time, to another century, where you are pulled by the rolling museum of Detroit. Old cars of your childhood—the ones when you started to drive oh so long ago—are here—now...in our Havana.

Noticeably missing in Havana are the billboards, malls and mega-stores from "the outside world." None of that exists in our blue Havana, and who needs it anyway? What could be a better way to alleviate the heat than strolling along the Malecón and feeling the sea breeze. And when the day ends, a distant radio plays old bolero, the Cuban version of old American blues standards with tales of lost loves. And the gentle sound of a game of dominoes with its enthusiastic and loud players—and the smell of rum. No ice, just straight, raw rum...

I worry about losing that old charm. More people are coming and going, they want better service, more modern hotels, American fast food, air-conditioned taxis. Many look for the typical tourist traps that are omnipresent across the Caribbean. They don't see the color of nostalgia, they want a home away from home.

Little by little, they will get their way, but there are some things that will not change in Havana: the smiling faces of the *habaneros*, proud of what they do and how they live, who will open their hearts as if they always knew you, and welcome you to their city.

Roberto Salas
Legendary photographer
of the Cuban Revolution (see pages 68-69).

Havana is changing at an alarming rate, yet stays transfixed in time. The past and the present could not mix better. To me, it is the most exciting place on Earth. As soon as I leave, I want to return: It is never enough.

I first stepped foot in Havana in 1989 and fell in love on the spot. I was charmed by the warmth and spirit of the people, amazed by their resourcefulness, drawn to the city's weathered beauty and otherworldliness. I had to keep coming back and I did. Each trip anchored me deeper and made me long for my adoptive city while away. Now I call it home, splitting my time between Cuba and Canada.

Havana is visceral—the sights, smell and sound. And ever so sensual. There is nothing like walking its streets and breathing in the life. You need to pinch yourself to believe the 360-degree panorama is real: the Cuban rhythms in surround sound as you stroll along, kids playing soccer barefoot in the plazas, the mosaic of humanity in the open doorways, and the exceptional beauty of the eclectic architecture that holds a surprise around every corner. Plus the smell of the black billowing exhaust from vintage cars permeating the city... only to be refreshed by the microclimates spattered around the city like the *Bosque de la Habana* (an urban jungle) and the windswept Malecón, the *habaneros'* miles-long seaside sofa.

It's only in Havana that you will discover: vintage American cars with Soviet engines; live music everywhere, even in the smallest venues; the *manicera* holding white paper cones full of peanuts chanting *maní*; locals ambling through town with ornate uncovered colorful birthday cakes, or dozens of eggs in open cartons; women walking to their day jobs in every variation of fishnet stockings, or striding confidently in hair rollers; the serendipity; the ubiquitous teal-blue hue.

No one looks you more in the eyes than in Havana. It is the city of stares, of sincerity and of kindness. People share, lend a helping hand, talk to each other, respect the elderly. They are affectionate— even complete strangers talk to each other in endearing terms—*Gracias mi amor* (Thank you my love) and *De nada mi vida* (My pleasure, my sweetheart).

Havana is a welcome respite from advertisements. This is the land of no brands.

Treasure your time here. And whatever you do, explore beyond the borders of beautiful Habana Vieja, to uncover the city's distinctive neighborhoods. That is what this book is all about, stepping into the unexpected: the explosive culinary scene, the ingenious artists, the intoxicating architecture, the natural wonders.

Here is my Havana.

Heidi Hollinger

MY TOP PICKS

TOP 10 MOJITOS
- La Guarida [#124]
- El Café (until 6 p.m.) [#7]
- O'Reilly 304 / El del Frente [#105]
- Melodrama [#4]
- Yarini [#56]
- Espacios—ask for the "Tobito" (biggest in town) [#222]
- paZillo [#202]
- Fábrica de Arte Cubano (FAC) [#207]
- Bleco [#122]
- ChaChaChá [#93]

BEST BREAKFASTS
- El Café [#7]
- Malecón 663 [#125]
- Color Café [#61]
- HAV Coffee & Art [#55]
- El Dandy [#2]
- Eclectico [#180]
- Fangio [#183]
- La Bodega de la Reserva [#192]
- El Gelato [#239]

ULTIMATE LUNCH
- Santy Pescador [#264]
- Antojos [#93]
- El del Frente [#105]
- Casa Mia [#187]
- Sensaciones [#244]

PIZZAHHH
- Bleco [#122]
- Espacios [#222]
- Marechiaro [#127]
- Meliã Habana "La Scala" [#252]
- Casa Italia [#225]
- 5 Esquinas [#91]
- Nero di Seppia [#225]

FOODIE'S DELIGHT
- Grados [#147]
- TocaMadera [#238]
- Santy Pescador [#264]
- Casa Italia [#225]
- Sensaciones [#244]
- La Cocina de Lilliam [#238]
- Musa [Avenida 3 #2404, btw 24 and 26; +535 081 6666]

VEGETERIAN / VEGAN FRIENDLY
- Camino al Sol [#174]
- Fonda Al Pirata [#101]
- El Café [#7]
- Hecho en Casa [#221]
- Café Bohemia [#25]

GLOBAL KITCHEN
- Casa Italia (Italian) [#225]
- Casa Miglis (Swedish) [#123]
- Buena Vista Curry Club (Indian) [#95]
- La Catrina (Mexican) [#216]
- Beirut (Lebanese) [#187]
- Nazdarovie (Soviet) [#127]
- Jama (Japanese) [#105]
- Marechiaro (Italian) [#127]
- La Bella Cubana, Meliã Habana (Japanese) [#252]
- Tien Tan (Chinese) [#118]

ROOFTOP TERRACES WITH A VIBE
- Bleco [#122]
- Yarini [#56]
- Malecón 663 [#125]
- Manteca [#121]
- El del Frente [#105]
- La Guarida [#124]
- El Cocinero [#208]

SUNSET DINING BY THE SEA
- Malecón 663 [#125]
- Arrecife [#230]
- Vistamar [#231]
- Santy Pescador [#264]
- La Divina Pastora [#279]
- Marea [#265]
- Amigos del Mar [#212]
- Nazdarovie [#127]
- Marechiaro [#127]
- Paseo Marítimo (aka 1ra y 70) [#236]

BOUNTIFUL WINE CELLARS
- Del Prado [#102]
- La Guarida [#124]
- Costa Vino [#181]
- PlanH [#102]
- Buena Vista Curry Club [#95]
- Il Divino [#275]

ICE CREAM
- El Gelato [#239]
- Café Enlace [#239]
- Ambrosia [#239]
- Dolce Neve [#239]
- Coppelia [#151]
- Mango (Teniente Rey #106, btw San Ignacio and Cuba)

LIVE MUSIC
- Fábrica de Arte Cubano (FAC) [#207]
- Café Teatro Bertolt Brecht [#171]
- Malecón 663 [#125]
- Yarini [#56]
- Coco Blue y la Zorra Pelua [#199]
- Café Solas [#5]
- Eclectico [#180]
- Casa de la Música Habana [#134]
- Casa de la Musica Miramar [#215]
- Claxon [#183]

NIGHTCLUBS
- Mio & Tuyo [#248]
- Don Cangrejo [#228]
- Johnny Club [#228]
- SangriLa [#248]
- EFE [#186]
- King Bar [#186]

MOVING SLOW
- El Bosque de La Habana [#213]
- San Isidro neighborhood [#56]
- El Callejón de Hamel [#134]
- Almacenes San José market [#51]
- Art Nouveau on Calle Cárdenas [#58]
- Calle Reina (from Galiano to Paseo de Martí)

ART DECO
- Edificio Bacardí [#84]
- López Serrano (Calle 13 #108, corner L)
- La Moderna Poesía (Calle Bernaza 527, corner Obispo)
- Teatro América (Calle Galiano 253, corner Concordia)
- Cine-Teatro Fausto [#217]

MY MUST-SEE MUSEUMS
- Museo de Bellas Artes / Edifício de Arte Cubano [#85]
- Centro Fidel Castro Ruz [#188]
- Museo de Artes Decorativas [#184]
- Castillo de la Real Fuerza [#69]
- Museo del Automóvil [#16]

CIGAR BARS / LOUNGES
- Casa del Habano: Partagas [#138], Meliã Cohiba [#200], Meliã Habana [#252], Club Havana [#263], Robaina 5ta y 16, Conde de Villanueva
- Hotel Nacional garden [#160]
- La Guarida [#124]
- Casa Abel [#126]
- Leales Cigar Lounge [by appointment only +535 868 4677 Peter]

COLLECTIBLE CUBAN CONTEMPORARY ART
- Fábrica de Arte Cubano (FAC) [#207]
- Galería Habana [#172]
- El Apartamento [#172]
- Galleria Continua [#117]
- Factoría Habana / Factoría Diseño [#107]
- Galería Taller Gorría [#56]
- José Fuster, Fusterlandia [#266] (contact Alex +535 281 5421)
- Galería Acacia [San José 114, btw Industria and Consulado; +537 863 1153]

ARTIST STUDIOS (BY APPOINTMENT)
- Manuel Mendive Hoyo [#223] (contact Alexander by WhatsApp +1 (786) 769-5556)
- Mabel Poblet [#148]
- Esterio Segura [#270]
- JEFF [#199]
- The-Merger Studio [#8]
- Liudmila & Nelson, Revolution Art Space (Calle 2, btw 35 and Paseo; revolutionartspace@gmail.com; +535 276 4677) [A p. 11]
- Gustavo Echevarría [#153]
- Roberto Salas for original prints of the revolutionary period [+535 268 6295]

HEMINGWAY TRAIL
- Finca Vigía [#276]
- Hotel Ambos Mundos [#72]
- La Bodeguita del Medio [#97]
- El Floridita [#82]
- Sloppy Joe's [#83]
- Marina Hemingway [#265]
- La Terraza [#286]

MY THRILL RIDES
- Classic convertible car ride, in English or Spanish, with Raúl Reyes León: +535 439 3697 [C]
- Electric bike tour with Martin Staub, Cubyke [#169]
- Boat ride along the Havana coast to the Morro with Alejandro Cordero [#265]
- Architecture tour with Luís Eduardo González Díaz [#218]
- Photography shoot around town with Osmel Azcuy: @osmelazcuy [B]

BEACHES / POOLS
- Santa María del Mar [#289]
- Tarará [#288]
- Club Havana [#263]
- Hotel Copacabana [#241]
- Marea [#265]
- Meliã Cohiba [#200]

Where to Stay

HABANA VIEJA
Large hotels
- Gran Hotel Manzana Kempinski [#86]
- Paseo del Prado [#87]
- The Grand Packard [#87]
- Gran Hotel Bristol La Habana [#86]

Boutique hotels
- Gardens, Havana [#9]
- Loma del Ángel [#67]
- Elvira, Mi Amor [#9]
- Jésus María 7 [#37]
- Loft Bahia [#37]
- A/S Boutique Residence [#55]
- Ánimas & Virtudes [#124]
- INNSiDE Habana Catedral [#99]
- Revolution Boutique Hotel [#94]
- Hostal Fresko [#67]

CENTRO HABANA
- Malecón 663 [#125]
- Tribe Caribe [#121]
- El Cuarto de Tula (San Lázaro 1063, btw Espada and San Francisco; +535 297 5700; www.elcuartodetula.com)

VEDADO
- Paseo 206 [#180]
- Claxon [#183]
- La Reserva [#192]
- Casa Brava [#192]
- Elegancia Suites Habana (Calzada 454, btw E and F; +535 354 6233)
- Meliã Cohiba [#200]
- Hotel Nacional [#160]

NUEVO VEDADO
- Chateau Blanc, first-of-its-kind kosher hotel in Cuba [Avenida Zoológico 103, btw 36 and 38; +535 812 7948; info@chateau-cuba.com] [D]

MIRAMAR
- Boutique Hotel Casa Italia [#225]
- Meliã Habana [#252]
- Grand Muthu Habana [#237]
- Villa Teresa (quaint rental, Avenida 1ra #3416, corner Calle 44; +535 388 8087)

GLOJJARY

GET TALKING
Que bolá? What's up? (slang)
Bien, gracias Fine, thanks.
Buenos días Good morning, or Hello.
Buenas tardes Good afternoon.
Buenas noches Good night.
Me llamo... My name is...
Puedo tirar una foto? May I take a photo?
Puedo pasar? May I go?
Disculpe Excuse me.
Hasta luego See you later.
Adiós Bye.
Cómo llego a...? How do I get to...?
Necesito la dirección de.... I need the address of...
Puede llevarme a esta dirección? Can you take me here (to this address)?
Cuanto cuesta? How much does it cost?
Donde está el baño? Where is the bathroom?
Un mojito por favor A mojito, please.
Dos cervezas por favor Two beers, please.
La cuenta, por favor The bill, please.
Primera vez en La Habana? First time in Havana? (People will ask you this.)
Quieres tomar algo? Would you like something to drink?
Quieres comer algo? Would you like to eat?
Soy vegetariano/a I am vegetarian.
Te gustaría bailar? Would you like to dance?

WORDS
Almendrón or **máquina** communal taxi
Avenida avenue
Cafetería snack bar
Calle street
Casa particular home or room to rent
Dale Hurry up, OK?
Farándula celebrities
Guagua bus
Guayabera men's short-sleeved cotton shirt with pockets
Habanero/a inhabitant of Havana
Lanchita ferry
Lindo/Linda beautiful
Museo museum
Orisha deity, spirit

Paladar privately owned restaurant
Parque park
Peña musical gathering or fiesta
Propina tip
Teatro theater
Yuma non-Spanish-speaking foreigner (slang)

FOOD and DRINK
Aguardiente unaged spirit made from sugarcane
Boniato sweet potato
Bonito tuna
Carne meat
Cerdo pork
Coco coconut
Comida criolla Cuban cuisine
Croquetas croquettes
Fruta bomba papaya (Don't say "papaya," Spanish slang for vagina.)
Guarapo sugarcane juice
Guayaba guava
Helado ice cream
Hierba buena mint
Mamey mamey sapote (a tropical fruit)
Maní roasted peanuts
Moros y cristianos black beans and white rice (Moors and Christians)
Papa potato
Papas fritas French fries
Pargo snapper (ubiquitous island fish)
Pescado fish
Piña pineapple
Pollo chicken
Ropa vieja pulled pork or shredded beef (literally, "old clothes")
Tostones deep-fried plantain
Yuca yucca, cassava

IF YOU HAVE AN ALLERGY
I am allergic...	**Soy alérgico/a...**
...to peanuts	**...al maní**
...to nuts	**...a los frutos secos**
...to seafood	**... a los mariscos**
...to gluten	**...al gluten**
I am lactose intolerant.	**No tolero la lactosa.**

USEFUL INFORMATION

Download maps.me on your phone BEFORE you go. It is a free OFFLINE GPS app for navigation. Make sure to also download the Cuba map that includes Havana.

Download WhatsApp, as most Cubans and restaurants use it to message.

Download La Nave App, a Cuban online taxi platform.

Download the Mandao App for food and grocery delivery services.

Bring cash as credit cards are not widely accepted (no credit cards issued in the United States are accepted). The most commonly accepted currencies are: the U.S. dollar, the Euro and the Canadian dollar.

Don't drink tap water unless it is boiled.

Watch where you walk. The *habaneros* know where all the holes in the streets and sidewalks are, but you don't.

Attention all foodies! The culinary scene is in full swing. Be sure to make a reservation: phone numbers are supplied in this book.

Tipping. Check your bill to see if service is included. If not, don't forget to tip.

Taxi. Agree on a fare up front. Meters are rare.

Ask for advice! Once in Havana, ask around about what live shows are on and which nights are best to go to particular venues. And check social media.

Health care. For hospitals for tourists, see page 139. **Osteopathy**: Roderic Hernández González [Calle 23 #809, corner A, Vedado].

Hairdresser. For all genders, Yoel Francis Suárez [Calle 4 #512, btw 21 and 23, Vedado].

Travel Agencies:
CubaPlus Travel (culture, adventure, wellness, eco-tourism, day trips), Nathali Soave, +535 992 0317, reservations@cubaplustravel.com;
In Cloud 9 (bespoke travel), Toby Brocklehurst, +4478019742657, info@incloud9.com;
San Cristóbal Travel Agency (historic tours of Old Havana), O'Reilly 102, corner Tacón, +537 801 7442.

Get familiar with Cuba before you go

Books: *Our Man in Havana* by Graham Greene, *The Old Man and the Sea* by Ernest Hemingway.

Movies: *Lucía, Fresa y Chocolate, Soy Cuba*

Street artist Fabián López aka 2+2=5?

HABANA VIEJA
Old Havana, South of Obispo

Extremely walkable with its narrow streets, you can feel the rhythm of the city at every step. Vintage American cars spot the roads where it is wide enough to drive, Spanish colonial mansions and colorful eclectic architecture line the streets. Old Havana has five main squares, three of which are south of Obispo Street. Originally enclosed by a stone wall, here you will find the traditional Jewish Quarter, the most beautiful church and the city's only mosque.

HABANA VIEJA

This Square is Anything but Square

1 Originally known as New Square when it was built in 1640, **Plaza del Cristo** is still the baby of the five main squares in Old Havana. It is the last one to be completely overrun by tourists and gentrified, which is why it has kept much of its charm. But that is all changing, as edgy new cafés and shops move in.

I love the feeling I get when I walk through the plaza: the human scale, the immersion into the daily Cuban landscape. There is energy, vibration, the place breathes life. Kids play soccer barefoot on the pavement, men sit on benches and play chess, lovers forget the world around them.

In the middle of the park there is a statue of Cuba's foremost romantic poet Gabriel de la Concepción Valdés (known as Placido), whose life came to a tragic end in 1844. On the northeastern edge of the plaza stands Iglesia del Santo Cristo del Buen Viaje, the church after which the park was named, and where sailors used to go and pray before embarking on a long journey.

Paladar means palate in both Spanish and Portuguese. It was the name of a restaurant in a Brazilian soap opera that was very popular in Cuba. Cubans coined the word for family-run restaurants in private homes at their onset in 1994; and later for all privately-run restaurants. *Paladares* originated during the *Período Especial* (Special Period), when the collapse of the Soviet Union led to the withdrawal of aid to Cuba.

Taking in the Scene

2 Perched on the corner of La Plaza del Cristo, **Café El Dandy** is a window to everyday life in Havana. The café-bar is named after a local gentleman who would dress up in an elegant suit and tie and stroll through Old Havana, stopping for photos with tourists—a large image of this adored "dandy" adorns one wall. El Dandy serves up pasta, tacos and breakfasts for champions. The loveable Angélica, with her ruby-red lipstick smile, delivers first-class espresso or a mojito—depending on the time of day. [Teniente Rey 401, corner Villegas; +535 395 2271]

Designed to be Cool

3 Opened in 2015 by Idania del Río and Leire Fernández, **Clandestina** became the poster child of Havana's emerging market economy.

At a time when it was difficult to find edgy souvenirs in Havana, Clandestina came to the rescue. It was the first contemporary design shop in the city—a breath of fresh air for trendy tourists as well as the discerning local consumer. The boutique is filled with silk-screen poster art, neon-inked T-shirts with witty slogans, as well as cool key chains, cups and caps. Everything is unique and manufactured in Cuba. Barack Obama bought a couple of their T-shirts for his daughters in 2016 when he was in town. Over the years I have amassed a sizeable batch: Beat the heat, have a Mojito!; Sensitive Enough; Nada es Perfecto; Resistir Vencer; Se Acabó El Drama; and Actually, I'm in Havana. At the cash, grab their prized Clandestina map of Old Havana musts.

All purchases are packaged in groovy brown paper bags. [Villegas 403, btw Teniente Rey and Muralla; shop online at clandestina.co]

Feeling creative? Go to their new space in the Almacenes San José (Reason #51) where you can design and print your own T-shirts while sipping an espresso or mandarin daiquiri while gazing out over the harbor.

The Cultural Café

5 Brothers Luis Carlos and Sergio Benvenuto Solás created **Café Solás** to pay tribute to Cuban artists in general, but particularly their uncle Humberto Solás, who is considered by many to be the father of Cuban filmmaking. Humberto, who directed the epic film *Lucía* during the 1960s, called the Golden Age of Cuban cinema, was also the mastermind behind the one-of-a-kind Festival de Cine Pobre de Gibara, the most culturally integrated film festival I have ever been to, founded in 2003 to showcase international low-budget digital films. Now back to the café! The extraordinary second-floor patio ensconced between stately colonial buildings is the stage for live music ranging from jazz to disco, and the scene for its weekly neighborhood movie club night. Grab a fresh strawberry daiquiri and browse the wall of photographs that highlights artists of all disciplines, such as author Alejo Carpentier (Reason #98), singer Omara Portuondo, dancers Carlos Acosta and Alicia Alonso, and visual artist René Portocarrero (Reason #13). [Cuba 159, btw Empedrado and Tejadillo; +535 400 0980]

Coziest Bar

4 A Swedish-Cuban joint adventure, **Melodrama** is one of the cutest and coziest bars in Havana, with undoubtedly the best name! Sit at the intimate bar where you have first-row seats on in-house creations like the Daiquirí Tiki, made of homemade guava juice and Cuban-spiced Havana Club dark rum. Order the black bean vegan tacos topped with veggies, and their outrageously addictive yuca fries served with aioli. Climb the staircase to a funky music-themed lounge with an extensive vinyl collection and try to catch an open mic session, where you can do your best Benny Moré. [Obra Pía 511, btw Bernaza and Villegas; +537 801 4193]

Undergarment Glory

6 **Cris-Cris**, a famous German seamstress from Berlin, left it all behind for her love of Cuba and opened her classy eponymous lingerie shop that looks out onto my beloved Plaza del Cristo. A treasure trove for lingerie lovers: sexy undies, bikinis, garters and *pareos,* all for a fraction of the price she would charge in Europe. Fabrics are sourced from Berlin and Mexico and all designs are made and produced by Cris-Cris with the help of a Cuban seamstress. Check out her new line of thongs called "Stringerie," sold in ornate tobacco boxes. [Villegas 361, corner Teniente Rey]

Decadent Breakfasts Made Fresh on the Spot

7 After six years of living and working in restaurants and cafés in London, Nelson Rodríguez Tamayo returned to Havana to open up a place of his own, simply named **El Café**. This trendy spot, set in a beautiful Spanish colonial building that took eight months of sweat and tears to renovate, with tables, chairs and a coffee machine brought by container ship from London, is the spot for everything fresh and local.

Superb coffee, freshly squeezed juice, be it guava, pineapple, carrot, ginger, beet or a combination, and decadent breakfasts with fried eggs (Cuban eggs are hands-down the best I've ever had), toast with homemade marmalade and artisanal bacon. And why not read a book and stay for lunch and have their fantastic hummus, veggie sandwich with grilled eggplant on their sourdough bread (a rarity in Havana!) and moist chocolate chip banana bread? Heck, stay for a late afternoon snack and try one of the best mojitos in Havana, made with special attention by Nelson and his dream team. The limes are squeezed with pure love and equal attention goes into muddling the *hierba buena* (mint) and the very emphatic rum pour! Open until 6 p.m. [Amargura 358, btw Aguacate and Villegas; +535 448 7003]

Mesmerizing, Smart, Edgy Art

8 **The-Merger Studio** is a collective of two incredibly talented Cuban artists whose work I adore: Alain Pino and Mario Miguel González. Primarily sculptors, they work with all sorts of materials, including stainless steel, bronze and Murano glass, to create stunning and sleek works of art that are always playful, but spiced with political or socioeconomic undertones. They use watercolor and oil paints as well as photography to create images that help guide them when making the sculptures; those images are works of art in themselves, and are often displayed together with the final creation. Walking into their gallery is like entering another dimension. It will take your breath away. [Monserrate 203, corner Tejadillo; +535 283 3492. Call Sandra for an appointment.]

9A

Dancers with African Roots

10 A group of **stilt dancers**, the *Gigantería*, often takes to the streets of Old Havana. It's hard to miss the 12-foot (3.65-meter) tall performers dressed in bright and colorful costumes gyrating to the Afro-Cuban rhythms of a conga. How they can strut the cobblestone streets on stilts is mindboggling.

The dance on stilts was brought to the island from Africa. The street-dancing troupe has joined forces with the Office of the City Historian in its aim to help preserve the culture and traditions that characterize Cuba by reviving Afro-Cuban street celebrations that were practiced several centuries ago by the people of the Villa San Cristóbal de La Habana.

Hotel Bliss

9 **Elvira, Mi Amor** (A) is the boutique hotel of two visionaries, Uri Bleier and José Capaz, set in a 1920s building that embodies that era's grandeur. Feast your eyes on furniture from the '50s and exclusive, space-specific installations by Cuban contemporary artists that defy traditional mediums. Try to book the room with a porcelain tub set smack in the middle draped with a floor-to-ceiling curtain transformed into a majestic painting by Capaz. [Compostela 565, btw Sol and Muralla; +535 842 7106]

Opened in 2019 by Jamie McDonald and Phil Winser, **Gardens, Havana** (B) isn't solely an eye-popping luxury boutique hotel. It represents a sanctuary of Cuban artistry where nearly every element, from furniture and lighting to tiles and artwork, is meticulously crafted by local artisans, even the new rooftop pool. Notable wall pieces by acclaimed artists, such as Damian Aquiles and Hector Frank, inspire. [Villegas 463, btw Muralla and Sol; +535 097 3178]

9B

11A

Tickle All Of Your Senses

12 Set in a captivating corner building in Old Havana near the Parque San Juan de Dios, **5 Sentidos**, "five senses" in Spanish, stimulates them all with mouthwatering tuna tartare, sautéed octopus and chicken masala. Towering windows flooding the space with light and the sleekest of interiors hung with crystal chandeliers transport you to early 20th century New York or Paris for the decadent and humming bistro feel. [San Juan de Dios 67, corner Compostela; +537 864 8699]

Advanced Mixology

11 **Lamparilla 361 Tapas y Cervezas** (A) [Lamparilla 361, btw Aguacate and Villegas; +535 390 8116] is a great spot for larger-than-life cocktails as well as tapas and beer—as its name implies. This adorable and funky restaurant, which opens fully onto Calle Lamparilla, draws you in with its colorful quirkiness and its 1950s memorabilia, and keeps you happy with exceptional service by its gregarious wait staff. Watermelon mojitos are a great way to beat the Havana heat; delicious starters include ceviche and chicken croquettes.

At the southern edge of the old city you'll find **Jíbaro** (B), where talented owner-mixologists Diana and David taught Prince Charles and Camilla how to make a mojito when the royal couple visited Cuba. You can stick with that Cuban classic, or take it up a notch and order an 8'as Kancha, a refreshing twist on Canchanchara, blending lemon, honey and a shot of 8-year Santiago rum. An eye-catching mural on the building helps you discover this off-the-beaten-path find. [Merced 69, btw Cuba and San Ignacio; +535 284 9545]

11B

THE VIRTUOSO OF VERSATILITY
Renowned Cuban architect **Orlando Inclán Castañeda**, known simply as Inclán, is the master at safeguarding Havana's architectural legacy, while simultaneously conceptualizing and seamlessly incorporating modern constructions. With his vision, colonial structures are undergoing a renaissance, evoking inspiration in all who enter. Embark on your own creative adventure by visiting his masterpieces: La Guarida #124, Malecón 663 #125, Yarini #56, Tribe Caribe #121, Habana 5 #91 (A sunset rooftop tour of these establishments, guided by Inclán, is available through Malecón 663 #125)

Poster Perfect

13 Check out this screen-printing workshop and gallery run by the Cuban Ministry of Culture and named after internationally renowned Cuban modernist artist René Portocarrero.

When you walk into this workspace with its industrial feel, it seems as if you are not supposed to be there, but it is indeed open to the public. You can see artists at work, art displays and hundreds of limited-edition screen prints for prices you'll love. Just ask the kind and keen staff of **Taller de Serigrafía René Portocarrero** to have a look; they will show you a treasure trove of vintage Cuban posters, in all styles and genres: music, art, photography, revolution related, etc. And if you are lucky, you can see the ancient—but still working—silk-screen tables and letterpress machines in use on some mornings. Fascinating. [Cuba 513, btw Teniente Rey and Muralla]

Where Function Meets Fashion

14 **Zulu** is a small boutique with unique leather bags, wallets and accessories made from leather recycled in-house. Gorgeous earthy tones, original shapes and exceptional quality give these items a distinctive cachet. This all-female family operation, founded in 1992 and run by Hilda Zulueta and her daughters Odamis and Mady, is winning awards worldwide for its singular sensations. [Aguacate 456, btw Teniente Rey and Muralla]

A Classy Concept Hotel

15 The elegant **Hotel Raquel**, named after Rachel, the matriarch of Jewish culture, was built in 1908 close to the Jewish Quarter of the city. A striking example of baroque and art nouveau, the building, renovated under the direction of Old Havana City Historian Eusebio Leal, had a former life as the headquarters of Cuba's main textile importer, and later, as the office and storage facility for the National Institute of Fisheries in the 1960s. When Soviet aid to Cuba ended in 1992, the structure was neglected. Today, the drop-dead gorgeous hotel is one of Old Havana's cherished treasures. I am astounded every time I walk into the lobby with its colossal columns and brilliant stained glass ceiling. The doorman is gracious and inviting. Bartender Rafael will mix up anything you desire in the lobby bar, aptly named **L'chaim** (Hebrew for "to life"). Check out the first- and second-floor rooms that, in keeping with the Jewish theme, are named after biblical figures like Leah, Hannah, Ruth, David and Solomon. And take the brass cage elevator to its decorative rooftop terrace for cocktails and snacks at the quaint bar. [Amargura 103, btw San Ignacio and Cuba]

Baby, You Can't Drive These Cars

16 Although Havana is a living car museum, at **Museo del Automóvil 'El Garage'** you can witness a selection of more than 50 historic vehicles frozen in time, like a very rare 1926 Rolls Royce Phantom 1, a 1956 Mercedes 190SL and 1959 Oldsmobile 98 driven by Cuban revolutionary Camilo Cienfuegos, and a popemobile from Pope Benedict's 2012 visit to Cuba. Don't miss the photo of María Calvo Nodarse, the first woman in the country to get a driver's license. I had a laugh when museum director Ignacio Reyes revealed why Cubans call early American cars "fotingos"—it stems from a phonetic translation of the Ford Model T slogan, "foot it and go." [San Ignacio 305-307-309, btw Teniente Rey and Amargura]

The Old Square

17 Beautifully restored **Plaza Vieja** is a must-see; it provides a magical glimpse into 16th-century Havana and a preview of what lies ahead for other parts of the old city. This square has had many names over the years and, like Plaza del Cristo, its first name was Plaza Nueva (New Square). Laid out in 1559, the square served as an open space for public events watched by the upper class from their balconies: executions, bullfighting and fiestas. In the 19th century it became Market Square and the commercial hub of the city. In 1952, then—President Fulgencio Batista had the outrageous idea to transform the square into an underground parking lot, demolishing the 18th-century fountain centerpiece by Italian sculptor Giorgio Massari in the process. After years of neglect, the square is once again abuzz thanks to the hard work of Old Havana's City Historian Eusebio Leal, the *Historiador* who restored the dilapidated structures back to their former glory and brought back

a replica of the fountain. Look for Roberto Fabelo's statue of a woman on a rooster, named *Viaje Fantástico* (Fantastic Voyage). Go for the view from the rooftop terrace at the recently renovated, ornate Palacio Cueto.

Education Comes First

18 **Angela Landa Primary School** in the heart of Plaza Vieja is an integral part of the neighborhood that adds character and authenticity: 400 schoolchildren use the square as their gymnasium and you can regularly see them playing baseball. This is a perfect example of how to do urban renewal in a historic center without killing the community. Few large cities have an elementary school smack in the middle of prime real estate. Havana is unique in this sense.

Will the government relocate the school as a result of gentrification? "They would never do that," says the school principal. "Education is too important in our society." With a literacy rate of more than 99 percent, Cuba puts education front and center.

It's hard to miss the wide-toothed cheery grins of the students in their ubiquitous burgundy school uniforms that are worn at all elementary schools across the island. [Teniente Rey 56]

A Map of Havana in Real Time

19 I absolutely love this place. On the top floor of the eclectic early 20th-century Gómez Vila building is a 360-degree view of Havana at **Cámara Oscura**. In this dark chamber, the image captured by an apparatus with strategically placed mirrors and lenses is projected in real time onto a concave platform. It's incredible to see this spontaneous map.

The presentation—in English or Spanish—lasts about 15 minutes and then you can go outside on the roof for a breathtaking view of Plaza Vieja and a chance to take some photos. Take the elevator to the top (8th floor). [corner Mercaderes and Teniente Rey]

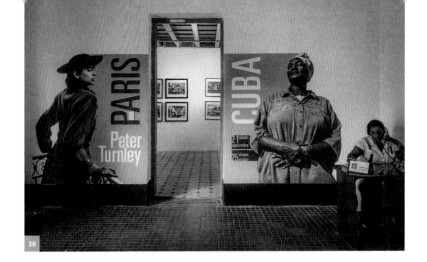

20

150 Years of Cuban Photography

20 **Fototeca de Cuba**, situated in the oldest building in Plaza Vieja, boasts the nation's largest collection of Cuban photographs. There is something magical about the place that has, since 1986, preserved and promoted Cuba's photographic heritage. It may be small, but every inch counts and you want to linger just a little longer. It hosts 12 exhibitions a year in its two galleries. Ground-floor Galería Joaquín Blez is mostly devoted to works by young up-and-coming photographers. Upstairs Galería María Eugenia Haya exhibits works by established Cuban and international photographers.

The Month of Photography, also known as *Noviembre Fotográfico*, is an event organized by the institution that coordinates shows in most of the galleries across Havana throughout November. During this time the Fototeca projects photographs from their collection onto the walls of the buildings in Plaza Vieja, which is quite impressive! [Mercaderes 307, btw Teniente Rey and Muralla]

The Jukebox

21 No wonder it is the most packed place on the plaza: **La Vitrola**'s camp, vintage decor with neon signs, model airplanes, antique bicycles and chandeliers hanging from the ceiling is the backdrop for great traditional Cuban food like *ropa vieja* and black beans. They have live music from lunchtime through dinner and serve an impressive Michelada. No word on whether Madonna drank one when she was there. [San Ignacio, corner Muralla; +535 951 8899]

21

Sweet Spot

22 Overlooking the square on the second floor is **Azúcar Lounge & Bar**. It is a great spot to take a coffee or piña colada break and watch the world walk by below. Try to get a table on the balcony for a supreme view of the 16th-century plaza or soak up the modern lounge feel inside and get ready for the live music. [Mercaderes 315, corner Muralla; +535 132 2451]

Ethical, Eco and Sustainable Fashion

23 For sophisticated simplicity with an island vibe head to **Dador**, an urban Cuban fashion and lifestyle brand designed by a collective of creative, socially conscious women led by Lauren Fajardo, Ilse Antón and Raquel Janero. Dador, the name taken from a poem by the famed Cuban writer José Lezama Lima, means "giver," reflecting the way this design group chooses to give back to its neighborhood by championing the "Made in Cuba" concept in the emerging Cuban private sector, and by adding socioeconomic value to the community. Their natural linen and cotton fabrics, and timeless versatile designs are the epitome of slow fashion. Their imaginative logo, a hot air balloon, is analogous to searching the horizon for new experiences. I mindfully display it when sporting my variety of Dador T-shirts. [Amargura 253, btw Compostela and Habana]

The Oasis
in the Old Square

24 Conveniently located in Plaza Vieja, **Spasio** is a refuge from the midday heat and throngs of tourists. One step inside this luxurious spa and you are in another world, starting with faux-Roman statues and columns. You can get a foot, full-body or couples massage in a dimly lit room with deep red regal tones, or do the water circuit to calm the nerves: Jacuzzi and steam room with eucalyptus aromas. When you emerge completely refreshed, put on your sunglasses as your eyes will need to adjust to the blaring sun beating down in the limestone plaza. [San Ignacio 364, btw Muralla and Teniente Rey; +535 353 9101]

People-Pleasing Menu

25 Named after *Bohemia,* a local arts and cultural magazine that has been an intellectual feast for readers for decades, **Café Bohemia** serves dishes rooted in organic farm products—tossing up Ensalada Bohemia and veggie Pizza Ortolana—as well as robust alternatives like the Sandwich Cubano, made with artisanal ham and grilled pork, with a side of *boniato* chips.

I like to sit and drink tea at their shaded tables right on the cobblestoned plaza, but don't miss seeing the offbeat restaurant interior, tucked away through an 18th-century archway opening up into a resplendent courtyard. Café Bohemia is also the venue of **Estancia Bohemia**—four uber-chic suites brought to you by the Italian-Cuban couple from Paseo 206 (Reason #180). [San Ignacio 364, btw Muralla and Teniente Rey; +535 243 1274]

How to Create Your Own Miniature Army

26 Just off Plaza Vieja you will find **Las Miniaturas De Arte**. This cute boutique sells tiny soldiers representing various historical eras of Cuban military struggle. In a small room behind the front counter, visible through glass, are artisans painting little lead soldiers—using large magnifying glasses and delicate paintbrushes. I was treated to an impromptu tour by Octavio the owner, who showed me the molds used to shape the platoons of tiny soldiers and the heating apparatus used to soften the lead.

With the influx of tourists, the demand for interesting and unique souvenirs has increased. To meet the changing tastes of their new customers, the shop recently started producing tiny lead figurines of some of Cuba's iconic personalities, including Che Guevara, José Martí and Ernest Hemingway.

Considering the work involved to produce these miniature masterpieces, they are a steal.

You can build up your own small Cuban army with the soldier waving the Cuban flag leading the charge. I love them! [Muralla 164, btw San Ignacio and Cuba]

Anyone for a Mojito?

27 With a name like **Mojito-Mojito** you better make amazing mojitos or else... And they do make a variety of the refreshing drinks. Top that with great live music, friendly professional service, beautiful atmosphere, yummy curry chicken, and you are in for a real treat. [Muralla 166, btw Cuba and San Ignacio; +535 510 6963]

Work Out with the Habaneros

28 If you want to work out while in Havana and are OK with a bit of grunge, this is an ideal spot to pump iron. Around the corner from Plaza Vieja, **Cuba Gym** is open to the public for a minimal entrance fee. Lose yourself in the past with the seemingly "prehistoric" gear; it may look rusty, but it does not hinder the muscle-making process—judging from the patrons of the gym. Get pumped! [Sol, btw Cuba and San Ignacio]

Perfect for Strolling

29 **Calle Mercaderes** is one of Old Havana's main streets that the *Historiador* of Havana restored in its entirety, building by building, reverting it back to the beautiful pedestrian cobblestone walkway it once was. The restoration was intended to be the prototype for the rest of the city. The second most traversed street in Old Havana after Obispo, Mercaderes (Merchants) street is where well-to-do families lived and where most of the merchants and commercial establishments were located. The street links Plaza de Armas with Plaza Vieja, making it one of the most culturally condensed streets in the city and an essential place to take a stroll.

Walking from top to bottom you can see the first university in Havana; the former governor-general's mansion; a plethora of mini-museums that preserve the former use of the buildings like the **Museo de los Bomberos** (Fire Station Museum); shops; the must-try and see Paladar los Mercaderes [Mercaderes 207, btw Lamparilla and Amargura; +537 801 2437] and a couple of teeny lush parks to catch some shade, including **Parque Simón Bolívar**, honoring Latin America's great liberator. At the end is **Café Taberna**, which is dedicated to Cuban music legend Benny Moré.

One-Stop Shop for Chocoholics

30 Along the fully restored Calle Mercaderes in Old Havana is a chocolate lover's paradise. Offering all things chocolaty, the **Museo del Chocolate** (Chocolate Museum), which also serves as a café, is your place to indulge. My friend Nelson, who is director of the Centro de Arte Contemporáneo Wifredo Lam (Reason #96) and a certified chocoholic, introduced me to this sweet spot. We both swear by the cold chocolate drink made with liquid chocolate and just a little milk. I routinely make a pilgrimage for this extraordinarily thick and decadent drink. For sale at the front cash are chocolate figurines such as dolphins, owls, violins, shoes, antique cars... There is something for everyone. You can watch as they make the artisanal chocolates on the spot. The air-conditioned room is an ideal place to escape the heat, but don't miss the little terrace hidden in back if you do not mind breaking a sweat. [corner Mercaderes and Amargura]

Churros Stand

31 Just in front of the Museo del Chocolate there is always a lineup at the **Churros** stand. Part of the fun is watching the process as the dough is lowered into the bubbling hot oil in one large swirl. When the big wheel of soft and crispy dough is taken out of the fryer, it is cut up with scissors, put in large paper cones and sprinkled with a weekly intake of sugar. [corner Amargura and Mercaderes]

Statuesque Street Art

32 Don't be surprised if you cross paths with a "statue" in Old Havana that might suddenly wink at you! These "**bronze sculptures**" are actually very elaborately made up and costumed mimes, who will pose tirelessly in the scorching Havana heat for photographers and selfie-seekers in exchange for a tip. One of my favorites is a guy I call "John Wayne."

Normally he likes to stand near the door of a bank (fashioning himself after a bank robber, no doubt) with his foot on a bucket and his hands resting on his pair of Smith & Wesson revolvers nestled into his holster. Drop some bills or coins into his bucket and he will immediately spring into action, drawing his revolvers and twirling them, menacingly pointing them in your direction. For his finale, he may lift the brim of his ten-gallon hat so that you can get a better look at his gold-toothed grin.

A Caring Convent

33 Another beautiful restoration project by Eusebio Leal (Reason #65) is the **Convento de Nuestra Señora de Belén** that introduced baroque architecture to the city in 1718.

In 1875, the world's first hurricane prognostic was given from the meteorological observatory inside. Today, the convent is a center for the elderly where the mission is to care for their health and well-being through cognitive stimulation, physiotherapy, optometry, healthy food, concerts and workshops—all for free, even new eyeglasses. It is also home to a preschool, giving children the opportunity to speak and bond with the elderly in the most peaceful of settings, with glorious arches and lush interior courtyard.

To visit, contact the **San Cristobál Travel Agency** (see page 15). No entry fee: donations welcomed. [Compostela 662, btw Luz and Acosta]

Sniffing Out Colonial Scents

34 Perfume has long been an important part of Cuban culture and at **Habana 1791**, aka **El Museo del Perfume**, you can see how the *habaneros* take their scents seriously. High-quality fragrances are made on-site from all-natural and local ingredients. You can sample, purchase and even create your own scent.

The perfume museum was established in 2000 by Yanelda Mendosa, who trained in the French perfume capital Grasse, in Provence. She recreates the olfactory past of bygone Havana with aromas of violet, lavender, jasmine, tobacco, coffee and leather, all in the opulent setting of a magnificent 18th-century colonial house.

Walk into antiquity and stimulate your senses, even if it is just to take a peek. [Mercaderes 156, btw Obra Pía and Lamparilla]

35A

Africa Lives Inside Every Cuban

36 African culture has had a definitive influence on Cuba's history, from tragic beginnings of enslavement to the rich beauty Africa has imparted on all levels: musical, social, religious, gastronomic, and scholarly. At **Casa de África** museum, you can witness a part of this momentous trajectory and see Fidel Castro's vast collection of gifts presented by African leaders, grateful recipients of Cuban aid. [Obra Pía 157, btw Mercaderes and San Ignacio]

Friday Prayers

35 **Abdallah Mosque** (A) became Cuba's first mosque when it was inaugurated in June 2015. Located in the heart of Old Havana, the mosque regularly receives some 200 worshippers for Friday prayers. Government acknowledgment of the mosque is noteworthy because being Muslim in Cuba is to renounce key parts of Cuban culture—eating pork, drinking rum and dancing salsa are no-no's. It's an interesting place for Muslim and non-Muslim visitors alike. [Oficios 13, btw Obispo and Obra Pía]

Right across the road from Abdallah Mosque is **La Casa de los Arabes** (B). An ethnographic museum that highlights Havana's great diversity, its permanent exhibits feature daggers, souks and objects of everyday Arab life in a grand setting with glorious archways and a courtyard fountain. Be on the lookout for the peacock, who likes to stop and pose when prancing about. [Oficios 16, btw Obispo and Obra Pía]

An Estampa Jewel

37 A *solar* in Cuba is a multifamily dwelling converted from what was a colonial home before the revolution. Set in such a building, the stunning boutique hotel-gallery-restaurant **Loft Bahia** (A) introduces design, art and style to this Old Havana *solar* while maintaining its charm. Three families still reside there. It is the vision of Estampa Collection, a project by Belgian architect Thomas Verwacht and Cuban attorney Susel Rodriguez to convert dilapidated properties into destination experiences: this one is a must-see. Wander up the grand staircase past sprawling art exhibits to the magnificent rooftop terrace for a panoramic view of Havana Harbor and one of the city's best brunches. [Oficios 402, btw Luz and Acosta; +535 401 1695]

Jesús María 7 (B) is an incredibly elegant and stunningly renovated boutique hotel with five spacious suites and a rooftop terrace overlooking the bay of Havana, where they serve their delicious breakfasts and sundowners. [Jesús María 7, btw Inquisidor and San Ignacio; +535 936 1266]

A Park for a Princess

38 On a trip to Havana, Mother Teresa asked the *Historiador* of the city if he would create a garden for Diana, Princess of Wales. A well-hidden haven, **Jardín Diana de Gales**, just north of Plaza de San Francisco de Asís, is an enchanting garden dedicated to her memory. This tropical park with a mesmerizing fountain featuring a 10-foot (3-meter) high Cubist column by acclaimed Cuban artists Alfredo Sosabravo and René Palenzuela, is perfect for a sentimental escape. The British Embassy funded the garden and also donated an engraved Welsh slate and stone plaque from Althorp, Diana's childhood home. Look up to see the crown on the wrought-iron gateway, a symbol somewhat at odds with revolutionary values. [Baratillo, btw Obra Pía and Oficios]

State-Run Swish

39 **Café del Oriente** is an opulent state-run restaurant in Plaza de San Francisco de Asís with a beautiful patio right on the square. Here, tuxedo-clad waiters serve filet mignon, accompanied by fine wines, and classical musicians perform piano concertos.

This is formal dining, Cuban-style, and you never know who you will run into. They have hosted Spanish royalty, and Raúl Castro chose it for a meal with Canadian Prime Minister Justin Trudeau. Don't miss the stained glass skylight on the second floor created by Cuban visual artist Rosa María de la Terga of Hotel Raquel fame (Reason #15). [Oficios 112, corner Amargura]

Where the Colonial-Era Sailors Hung Out

40 The second of the five squares built in Old Havana, **Plaza de San Francisco de Asís** was, in the early 17th century, the main commercial hub. The crews of Spanish galleons would load up on rum, cigars, beans and rice, sell enslaved people and watch cockfights until irate wealthy locals convinced authorities to move the scene to Plaza Vieja.

Sit at the lion fountain and watch pigeons fly through the plaza in dizzying circles. Their swift and fantastical movements make for great photographs with the backdrop of the **Basílica Menor de San Francisco de Asís**, or with the stunning **Lonja del Comercio** (the stock exchange building). Look up to see a replica of Florence's statue of Mercury on its roof. At the east end of the square is a statue of Frédéric Chopin sitting on a bench; have a seat with him.

Since colonial times, the plaza has been the starting point for religious pilgrimages at Easter. Today, a new sort of pilgrim is emerging—young *quinceañeras* in colorful taffeta dresses celebrate their 15th birthday in style, with an obligatory stop at the plaza.

Located just behind the basilica is a little island of serenity, the **Mother Teresa of Calcutta Garden**, where a sweet sculpture of her sits on a bench. The garden is also home to **St. Nicholas Greek Orthodox Church**, and a small cemetery called Campo Santo where lay the ashes of the beloved Eusebio Leal (Reason #65).

The Sound of Music

41 Enjoy the incredible acoustics of **Basílica Menor de San Francisco de Asís**, a 16th-century church that hosts live classical music performances at 6 p.m. every Saturday (there is a new program every week). Their exceptional concert series is an initiative to promote culture in some of the city's unique places. The basilica is home to the renowned all-female chamber orchestra, Camerata Romeu, which left me in awe. You cannot miss the painting behind the stage; it depicts a shepherd holding a child that I find bears a striking resemblance to Fidel Castro! [Oficios and Amargura]

Rub His Beard for Good Luck

42

For good luck I always stop and rub the beard and hand of the bronze statue **El Caballero de París** right in front of the Basílica Menor de San Francisco de Asís. Mind you, this is not always an easy feat as often there are already hordes of tourists or school children that have swarmed the statue and have positioned themselves for selfies with the legendary figure.

El Caballero de París was a real person who, for over four decades, roamed the streets of Havana dispensing stimulating conversation and philosophy to all who would approach him. He was easily recognizable with his long salt-and-pepper beard, and his wild, unkempt gray hair, long curly fingernails and an elegant black cape that he would wear no matter how hot it might be. Although he was considered a "street person," he never asked for money and only accepted offerings in exchange for little crafts that he made.

At one point (he died in 1985 at the age of 86), almost all *habaneros* had a story about an encounter they had with him, be it near Plaza de Armas, on the Paseo del Prado, in Parque Central (where he was known to have slept on benches), on 5th Avenue in Miramar or riding a bus.

Born José María López Lledín in 1899 into a wealthy Spanish family, El Caballero immigrated to Havana at the age of 12. He worked as a store clerk and then at Hotel Inglaterra and at Café París on Obispo.

There have been many rumors about the origin of his nickname. He told his biographer that "El Caballero de París" comes from a French novel.

Others say that when he worked at Café París, he began proclaiming to be a gentleman and a king, and the patrons started to refer to him as the "Caballero de Paris." Some family members have stated that it was his Parisian sweetheart who had given him the nickname.

Following his death, he was initially buried in the cemetery of Santiago de Las Vegas in Havana but, at the behest of Old Havana's City Historian Eusebio Leal, his remains were exhumed and then transferred to the Basílica Menor de San Francisco de Asís. A bronze sculpture by José Villa Soberón, who also sculpted John Lennon's statue in Parque John Lennon, in Vedado (Reason #195), was later installed to commemorate the memory of this cherished public figure. [Oficios, btw Amargura and Teniente Rey]

A Gallery for Cuban Artists

43 Step inside **Galería Carmen Montilla** and behold the incredible 3-D mural by famed Cuban artist Alfredo Sosabravo at the end of the garden courtyard. When you get closer to the huge ceramic-tiled puzzle, spot the fish, birds and fruit, all permanent motifs of his work.

This adorable art gallery, established in 1994 by the late Venezuelan artist Carmen Montilla, is housed in an 18th-century building where her works—and that of contemporary Cuban and Latin American artists—are exhibited. Check out Havana's only sculpture of Mozart, given to the Cuban people as a gift by the city of Salzburg. [Oficios 162, btw Amargura and Teniente Rey]

Pious Pause

44 This curious hotel has a monastic theme, with staff sometimes dressed as friars who greet you at the entrance. **Hotel Los Frailes** was never a monastery, but the Franciscan friar thing was inspired by the proximity of Basílica Menor de San Francisco de Asís—it's just around the corner. The hotel is literally a cool place to zip in for a drink at the lobby bar before heading back out into the frenzied heat. Kick back in the cozy couches and listen to a string quartet for a moment of tranquility.

Check out the lush inner courtyard with hanging vines and a view of an original *aljibe* (water cistern) that was uncovered during extensive renovations to the hotel; the same type of limestone cisterns are located under the courtyard of every colonial mansion in Old Havana. [Teniente Rey 8, btw Mercaderes and Oficios]

Havana Time

45
Watch collectors will not want to miss **El Reloj Cuervo y Sobrinos**, an elegant art deco boutique museum that showcases watches and other luxury items from the prestigious Cuervo y Sobrinos watchmakers, a brand founded in 1882. The timepieces are crafted with a unique blend of Cuban design and Swiss watchmaking expertise. In the 1940s, this landmark was a must-stop for international celebrities visiting Havana, including Ernest Hemingway, Enrico Caruso, Clark Gable, Winston Churchill and Albert Einstein. As a reprieve from the heat, you can soak in the prestige of this unique brand and its history while taking a coffee break or a timeless cocktail at the bar at the back. [Oficios, corner Muralla]

The Language of Rum

46
Welcome to the **Museo del Ron Havana Club** (A) for a guided tour that takes you behind the scenes of the rum-making process. The first part of the visit focuses on how and why sugar cane stalks were introduced to Cuba; next, you actually get to see how Havana Club rum is produced. The tour ends with a tasting session propelled by live Cuban musicians. Offered in five different languages—Spanish, English, French, German, Italian—you might end up speaking them all after the tasting! [Avenida del Puerto 262, corner Sol]

Just around the corner is the tiny, charming **L'Antigua Habana** (B) filled with antique books, old *Bohemia* magazines, jewelry, vinyl... It is a true time capsule. [Santa Clara 10A, btw Oficios and Avenida del Puerto]

A Legendary Watering Hole

47 Opened in 1894 by two brothers from Spain, **Restaurante Dos Hermanos** has seen it all. Facing the port, this was a regular haunt for rum-soaked sailors, gangsters and Hollywood stars, including Marlon Brando and Errol Flynn. Writers Federico García Lorca, Alejo Carpentier (Reason #98) and Ernest Hemingway "have all raised their glasses here to friendship and the joys of life" reads the plaque on the wall. Graham Greene was a regular when he traveled to the capital. The exquisite hardwood bar is described in the novel *Fiebre de Caballos* (Horse Fever) by Leonardo Padura (Reason #272), in which the young protagonist sits at the bar receiving words of wisdom on growing up, surrounded by drunks and alluring women.

When I walk through its swinging doors, the live music and the backdrop of the timeless bar immediately transform my mood. And that is even before sampling their spirited cocktails! [Avenida del Puerto 305, corner Sol]

Waterfront Cathedral

48 A long-standing dream for the many Russian faithful living in Cuba was realized when the **Catedral Ortodoxa Nuestra Señora de Kazán** (Our Lady of Kazan Russian Orthodox Cathedral) was consecrated in 2008. The project initiated by Fidel Castro himself as a testament to Cuban-Russian friendship also coincided with the renewal of Cuban-Russian relations. The impressive Byzantine-style cathedral overlooks the ocean, making it a key part of Havana waterfront architecture. Take a look inside to see beautiful ornaments, bells and crosses brought from Russia. [Avenida del Puerto, btw Sol and Santa Clara]

Don't Miss the Boat

49

One of Havana's "cheap thrills" is to hop on the **lanchita** (ferry)—to either Regla or Casablanca, two districts across the harbor from Old Havana. It costs next to nothing (a few cents), but the ride is *priceless*.

For a multitude of reasons, Cuba is an island with a dearth of boats, which means that scenic boat cruises along Havana's coast are not common. However, those in the know can take a boat tour (of sorts) by climbing aboard the *lanchita*.

It is a form of public transit for locals, and for visitors it is a unique opportunity for a breathtaking view of Old Havana from the water.

The ferries are a bit run down, but being on board gives you a chance to see a slice of life in Havana—an elderly man with his bicycle stacked high with crates of eggs, kids running to get a window view (you should, too!) and lovers embracing,

looking out at the sunset with wind in their faces.

Watch your step when getting on and off; there is a huge gap between the *lanchita* and the dock. See the chapter on Casablanca and Regla to see what to do when you get there. El Emboque de Luz ferry terminal is right across from Hotel Santander. [Avenida del Puerto, corner Luz].

A Pub with a Panoramic View

50 Waterfront renewal by the Office of the City Historian is bringing about beautiful changes to the shoreline. One colossal undertaking was the **Cervecería Antiguo Almacén de la Madera y el Tabaco** beer hall, which serves up to 400 guests at any given time. It is located on a pier in a recently renovated former lumber and tobacco warehouse. On the patio in the front sit a historic train engine, coal car and caboose.

Here you can order a *tarros*, Havana's famous chilled beer towers from which you can self-pour 100 ounces (three liters) of locally-crafted beer. They also serve up Cuban specialties from their gigantic indoor grill and have live music playing, which inevitably leads to spur-of-the-moment salsa dancing. [Avenida del Puerto and San Ignacio]

Artisans' Square Mile

51 Havana's biggest craft market is located in a restored port warehouse the size of an airplane hangar; **Almacenes de San José** (San José Market) (A) [Avenida del Puerto and Cuba] has everything under the sun. Guayaberas galore, Che Guevara T-shirts, a full spectrum of whimsical art, fun jewelry. I wear my Cuban flag earrings whenever I get the Havana blues. In the middle of the market, there is a coconut seller who can hack open a huge green "coco" with his machete and carve out the flesh after your last sip. There is an option for a rum pour. In the way that Cubans do, we exchange terms of endearment. I say *gracias mi amor* (thanks, my love), to which he replies *de nada mi vida* (you're welcome, my sweetheart). Climb upstairs for a serious brew at **Sabor Café**, a coffee shop from bean to cup owned by barista Fanette Arteaga Romero. Also shop at Clandestina's (Reason #3) new workshop and café-bar, or Fresko's (Reason #67) sweet boutique.

After you're done souvenir shopping, stop in across the street at the incredibly cool **Pacos Mar** (B) [Cuba 902, btw San Isidro and Desamparado; +535 916 3131] for shrimp tacos and their two-story-high daiquiri.

Cuban One-Two Punch

52 When I walked into the **Rafael Trejo Boxing Gym** in Old Havana, 10-year-old boys were slugging it out in the ring. They were ferocious! It was surreal to see the intrepid pint-sized fighters with their oversized boxing shorts, worn-out boxing gloves and nifty haircuts pounding at each other until the bell rang. This scene constantly plays itself out on weekends when young boxers compete in sanctioned matches in the hope that they will climb up the rankings.

Success at this gym can propel fledgling careers up the first-rate Cuban boxing program in a country where local athletes in this sport include some of the best in the world. These kids are serious and nothing is standing in their way of a gold medal somewhere down the road! Like much in Havana, you need to see it to believe it! [Cuba 815, btw Merced and Leonor Pérez]

51B

52

Ecclesiastical Wonder

53 This may look like any other baroque church from the outside, but wait until you have a look inside **Iglesia y Convento de Nuestra Señora de la Merced**. Built in 1867, its magnificent interior makes it an absolute must-see when in Havana. Appreciate the most outstanding collection of religious frescoes and paintings by renowned 19th-century Cuban artists. This is a real beauty. [Cuba 806, btw Merced and Leonor Pérez]

the bay at Fortaleza de San Carlos de la Cabaña (Reason #279) alerted citizens that the gates were closing for the night and that they should be inside! Demolished in 1863, vestiges of the wall can be seen at Museo de la Revolución (Reason #88) and also on Avenida de Bélgica, close to the train station, itself a national monument for its eclectic architectural style with its two high towers and decorative Spanish-style inspiration.

Get In or Stay Out

54 To protect the city from pirates during the 17th century, *Habana Vieja* was enclosed by a three-mile (five-kilometer) long **city wall**, built by enslaved people from Africa, with heavily guarded gates. Every night the sound of a cannon shot fired from across

Hombre es más que negro, más que mulato y más que blanco.
(Man is more than black, more than mulatto and more than white)
José Martí

The Apostle of Cuban Independence, and a Divine Way to Start the Day

55 You won't be able to take five steps in Havana without coming across a tribute to **José Martí**, Cuba's national hero. He is in the hearts and minds of all Cubans. Born in Havana in 1853, Martí dedicated his life to, and was the driving force behind, Cuba's struggle for independence from Spain. Martí thought it preposterous that Cuba be controlled and oppressed by the Spanish government when it had its own unique identity and culture. He was a poet and an intellectual whose main themes of freedom and liberty ran across all his works. He died fighting in the Cuban War of Independence in 1895 at the age of 42. But before Martí died, he put out a book of poems titled *Versos Sencillos* (Simple

Verses), which is for many Cubans like a bible. It is a magnificent body of work; try to get your hands on a copy!

The house where he was born was converted into a museum in 1925. **El Museo Casa Natal de José Martí** (A), where you can see fascinating photographs and exhibits, focuses on different stages of his life. [Leonor Pérez 314, btw Avenida de Bélgica and Picota]

A few blocks away, **HAV Coffee & Art** (B) inside **A/S Boutique Residence** [Jesus María 258, btw Compostela and Picota; +537 861 2898] is a must-witness taste and experience passion project by couple Cuban dancer and musician Sandy Solano Díaz and Dutch abstract artist and fashion guru Andre Visser. The fusion of old world and contemporary design makes for an exquisite mix in this six-room dreamy boutique hotel, café and gallery. Feel the dramatic effect of the 16-foot ceilings and wall to wall evocative contemporary art during your organic breakfast or lunch escapade in one of Havana's most exciting emerging neighborhoods.

After years of anticipation, the larger-than-life resto-bar **Yarini** (A) opened above GTG, owned by Adán and run by a rocking crew. This sizzling hot spot comprises a luxuriant rooftop restaurant with a sky-high bar serving Cuban international cuisine and an upper-upper bar for the cool crowd. It quickly became a hub for Cuba's top recording artists and DJs from around the world. Alberto Yarini, its namesake, was a famous Cuban racketeer and pimp who acted as a kind of Robin Hood in Havana during the 19th century. Pichi, along with his family, have been contributing to the redevelopment of this special district in Old Havana and is a kind of Robin Hood in his own right. [San Isidro 214, btw Picota and Compostela; +535 897 9835]

San Isidro, Embellished

56

Cuban star Jorge Perugorría (aka Pichi) (Reason #257) is more than an actor, he is an accomplished visual artist and a community-minded benefactor. With the help of Eusebio Leal (Reason #65), he opened **Galería Taller Gorría** and turned a dilapidated bakery on Calle San Isidro—in a neglected part of Old Havana—into an edgy arts cooperative. Run by Pichi and his son Adán, GTG's mission is to bring some much-needed attention to the neighborhood by promoting local artists and displaying their work. Through GTG's initiative, the whole district has become like a little Wynwood, with street art on every corner by artists, including Mr. MYL, 2+2=5? and ABSTRK.

Jewish Havana

57 In the old Jewish Quarter, in the southern part of Old Havana, there remains the city's only orthodox synagogue, **Sinagoga Ortodoxa Adath Israel**. Old Havana was the center of its cultural and commercial activities: kosher butcher shops, bakeries, warehouses of imported goods, and publishing houses. On Calle Obispo, there was a tailor shop founded in 1875 that doubled as a meeting place designed to help newly arrived Jewish immigrants begin a new life.

The Jewish community in Cuba dropped from 20,000 pre-revolution to about 1,200 today; most live in Havana. When Cuba changed its constitution in 1992, and began allowing religious freedom, the Jewish community started to rebuild. Now with three synagogues in total (**Beth Shalom** and **Centro Hebreo Sefaradi** Reason #170) the Jewish community is very tightly knit and free to practice its religion. While none of the congregations has their own rabbi, visiting rabbis from all over the world come regularly to celebrate important holidays and events. [Picota and Acosta]

Jewish History in Cuba

There are five synagogues in Cuba—three in Havana, one in Santiago, and a newer one, in Camaguey, built in 1998. There are also community centers that double as synagogues in Santa Clara and Guantanamo, and some homes in Manzanillo, Campechuela, Cienfuegos and Sancti Spiritus are used to worship.

The Cuban Jewish community dates back centuries. The first Jew to come to Cuba was among Christopher Columbus' 1492 crew. He later converted to Catholicism. Some Cubans trace their ancestry to Marranos, who fled Spain during the Inquisition. It is said that Isabel de Bobadilla, the face of the Giraldilla statue—the symbol of Havana—was eventually identified as a Sephardic Jew.

The largest wave of Jewish immigrants to Cuba came from Eastern Europe in the 1930s.

Ser culto es el único modo de ser libre.
(Being educated is the only way to be free)
José Martí

Art Nouveau on Calle Cárdenas

58 There is one particular street that most artists, architects, art directors and set designers make a beeline to when they arrive in Havana and that is **Calle Cárdenas**. This street features some of the best examples of art nouveau architecture *anywhere*. In fact, many master's dissertations have been written specifically on this urban beauty that fights the ongoing battle between decay and original glory. Just south of the Capitolio Nacional (Reason #111), Cárdenas begins at Máximo Gómez and extends five blocks to the train station.

Two addresses especially stand out: #103 and #107. If decorative architecture turns you on, like it does me, be prepared to have weak knees on Cárdenas. [Cárdenas, btw Máximo Gómez and Arsenal]

Gone but Not Forgotten

59

Hotel Saratoga was one of Havana's most elegant hotels. Superbly located on Paseo de Martí and Dragones, on the edge of Old Havana, it was one of my favorite buildings in the city with its mint-green facade; it was reminiscent of New York City's Flatiron Building, only shorter and wider. The main lobby was lavish with Spanish antiques, the mezzanine above opened into a glorious art nouveau lounge that screamed "ladies who lunch," and the dining room served up a buffet breakfast that had few peers. The rooftop pool had a South Beach vibe, replete with cabana boys in navy shorts and white polos. The Saratoga drew top-tier guests, including Mick Jagger, Jimmy Page, Jay-Z and Beyoncé. Then on May 6th 2022, the landmark 1880s building was destroyed by an accidental explosion. The memory of this peerless grande dame, however, remains.

What to bring home from Havana

RUM Santiago de Cuba 11 years was my longtime favorite, but now that Eminente has come along... Havana Club 7 años is an all-time classic and you can't ignore the new kid in town, Black Tears.

CIGARS Buy only in the state-run stores to avoid fakes. (See Reason #138)

CONTEMPORARY ART Find incredible, collectible visual art in my Top Picks (page 12). And artful items from design shops where form and function collide. (See Reasons #3, 6, 23, 61, 106, 125).

A Simply Majestic Theater

60

The Office of the City Historian went to great lengths to restore **Teatro Martí**, a Romanesque-style theater that was closed to the public for nearly 40 years. Built in 1884, this home of satirical musicals reopened in 2014. It was considered top priority to bring the theater back to life, not only for its neoclassic architectural value, but also for being the mecca of Cuba's *teatro bufo*, satirical plays that once mocked Spanish authority. Teatro Martí is where Lizt Alfonso Dance Cuba (Reason #110) performs. Try to catch a show while in town. [Dragones 58, btw Paseo de Martí and Agramonte (Zulueta)]

A Passion for Flavor and Fashion

61 Walking the narrow streets of Old Havana, there is no end to the gems you will find along the way, shining bright among weathered structures. In 2019 **Color Café** became one of them, created by gifted clothing designer Loypa Izaguirre, part of the new wave of entrepreneurs turning Havana into a design hub. Lined with her Cuban-inspired attire made from colorful French linen, silk and cotton, you can shop until you drop into a vintage 1950s Harry Bertoia chair to rejuvenate with a fresh smoothie like the Verde Verde, made of pineapple, cucumber, spinach, ginger and honey. Open early for breakfast (shoutout!) you can dig into a plate of *huevos rancheros* served with homemade hot sauce, which, as Loypa attests, is particularly effective for hangovers. [Aguiar 109, btw Chacón and Cuarteles; +535 970 9549]

Pizza, Pizza

62 The pizza in this tiny Italian eatery is amazing and affordable. The thin, crispy crust at **Venamí** comes with the perfect proportion of sauce, cheese and toppings. And you can add spices and their homemade pesto found on each table. Right in between the Capitolio and Plaza del Cristo, this family business is a great place for a quick bite. It's tiny, but full of heart. Take the kids! They will love it. [Monserrate 435, btw Teniente Rey and Lamparilla]

Roberto Salas

The Heart of Havana

63

Many consider **Parque Central** (A) to be the epicenter of Havana. Tucked in between the districts of Old Havana and Centro Habana, the park is a lush city square featuring wrought-iron benches, lampposts and a centerpiece statue of the ubiquitous national hero and apostle of Cuban independence, José Martí (Reason #55).

Listen in on the fiery debates taking place at **La Esquina Caliente** (B) (the Hot Corner), where local baseball fans argue feverishly about statistics and players' attributes well into the evening; watch ballerinas stretch before the curtain call at the Gran Teatro (Reason #113); jump onto the Hop On, Hop Off double-decker bus idling noisily as it awaits its next departure; grab a bus to the beach (Reason #289), and hail a convertible classic car to take you on a tour of the city.

Head up to the rooftop terrace of Hotel Parque Central [Agramonte 267] for one of the best vistas of the park. And grab a cold one!

Collector Car Cabs

64

A taxi in Havana is like a moving museum. Almost any car can be a cab so if you stick out your hand you might end up getting a lift in a bulky 1940s Chevy, a pink Cadillac from the '50s, a miniature Polski Fiat or a boxy Soviet Moskvich. I've ridden them all! Equally surreal are the retro interiors that are just as mesmerizing as the **vintage cars** themselves.

Fidel Castro outlawed the purchase of foreign cars after the revolution and for over 50 years—with the exception of Soviet and Eastern European cars sold at subsidized prices—Cubans had to make do with the wheels they had. And how do the cars keep rolling? Cuban ingenuity! You will find American classics fitted with Russian diesel engines, sometimes from tractors. Most drivers will insist on helping you open and close the doors in an effort to help preserve the fragile cars and because sometimes it only works with the flick of *their* wrist. And don't expect to find a seatbelt...

Haggling is often a part of the experience and since most taxis are not metered it's better to fix a price before getting in. And if the price isn't right, another vintage marvel is always just around the corner.

Page 68
Roberto Salas, my dear friend and one of the epic photographers of the early revolutionary period (1959-1964). For original prints contact Roberto. [+535 268 6295]

The Refurbishing Wizard: Eusebio Leal

65 **Dr. Eusebio Leal Spengler** was one of the most important people in the modern history of Havana. He was the *Historiador* (City Historian) and was in charge of the restoration and preservation of the Historic Center of Havana from 1981 until his death in 2020 at age 77. Buildings that had been falling apart after years of neglect were renovated and colorfully repainted one by one under his supervision. Many of these structures became hotels, restaurants, shops, museums and theaters, that helped pay for future restorations. Each project began by understanding how it would mesh with the community. Leal's first preoccupation was always what is best for Havana, the city about which he was so passionate.

He somehow managed to be everywhere at once, took care of everyone, and was admired and revered by all. He could often be seen walking the streets, in his signature gray pants and shirt, always ready for business. He was the right person at the right time to lead the way for this remarkable city into its promising future. For this reason alone, Havana is one lucky place.

Learn more about his life's work by visiting **La Casa de Eusebio Leal** [Amargura 65, btw Mercaderes and San Ignacio], or contact San Cristóbal Travel Agency [O'Reilly, corner Tacón; +537 801 7442] for a private walking tour of his transformations in Old Havana. You can pay homage to this exceptional person, and my treasured friend, in the Mother Teresa of Calcutta Garden next to Plaza de San Francisco de Asís (Reason #40), where he was laid to rest.

HABANA VIEJA
Old Havana, North of Obispo

This is where, in 1519, the city was founded along the bay, whose shape gave it natural protection for its Spanish galleons and colossal treasures. It is the area most frequented by tourists with its cobblestoned roads, the first castle—Castillo de la Real Fuerza, the earliest square—Plaza de Armas, the oldest churches and the Havana Cathedral in Plaza de la Catedral. You will find classic bars like la Bodeguita del Medio alongside the new generation of cocktail shakers at El del Frente, and the most spectacular expression of art deco in the city—the Bacardí building. Old Havana was named a UNESCO World Heritage site in 1982.

The First of Old Havana's Five Squares

66 The city's oldest square, **Plaza de Armas**, was built shortly after the town of San Cristóbal de La Habana was founded in 1519. It is the historic heart of the city as everything grew from here.

The square has incredible royal palms and kapok trees, which produce cooling shadows that counter the sweltering heat. A statue of independence hero Carlos Manuel de Céspedes is the oft-photographed centerpiece, while the Cuban baroque Palacio de los Capitanes Generales (Reason #68) and Palacio del Segundo Cabo, both built in the 1770s, are stunners. The latter was constructed by the Spaniards as a post office and communication center for their colonies. The name of the square was adopted in the 16th century when it was used as a military training ground—*armas* means weapons. Seville, Santiago and Lima each have their own Plaza de Armas, but I think that Havana's is the most beautiful.

Silence of the Loma

67 When Jodi Foster and her family stayed at **Hotel Loma del Ángel** (A) in 2017 with her family, she asked to see the owner, Eulalia "Lali" Pérez de Lucia, because she just had to meet the person who created the magical boutique hotel. This chic and stylish two-suite, five double-room sanctuary beside tiny Plaza del Ángel is prized for the classy architectural overhaul of this historic colonial building, its impeccable fusion of contemporary and vintage styles and its breathtaking rooftop views. [Cuarteles 104, corner Habana; +535 515 1525]

An adorable boutique hotel with a creative clothing line to boot, **Fresko** (B) is fun, funky and right in the heart of the action. [Callejón Espada 4, btw Chacón and Cuarteles; +537 801 5251]

Cuban Baroque

68

You can't miss **Palacio de los Capitanes Generales** on the eastern flank of Plaza de Armas. A magnificent example of 18th-century Cuban baroque-style architecture, the palace was the residence of Cuba's 65 colonial governors. Note the unique wooden cobblestone bricks in front of the palace—they were placed there by special request of one governor to muffle the click-clack sound of passing horse-drawn carts so that he would not be disturbed during his daily nap! The surface needs to be changed every two to three years.

The palace has served various functions over the centuries and is now home to the Museo de la Ciudad (City Museum). It's definitely worth taking the time to see the lavish interior and beautiful tree-filled courtyard with its marble statue of Christopher Columbus. [Tacón, btw O'Reilly and Obispo]

Love is in the Air

69 The oldest stone fortress in the Americas and the best example of Renaissance military architecture is **Castillo de la Real Fuerza** (Castle of the Royal Force); it was built from limestone extracted from the nearby Havana shoreline.

It was erected between 1558 and 1580 after the notorious French pirate Jacques de Sores, in 1555, set the original wood construction aflame and looted Havana before sailing off.

On top of one of the towers facing north toward the sea is the first bronze statue in Havana and the symbol of the city, La Giraldilla: a weather vane with a sculpture of a woman, replicating the figure crowning La Giralda in Seville. What I love about the statue is the romantic undertones surrounding it. Legend has it that the face of the statue is that of Isabel de Bobadilla, the wife of Hernando de Soto, Cuba's 8th governor, who was appointed by the Spanish Crown to conquer what is today Florida. He died during the expedition, but it is said that his wife, unaware that he had died, climbed the tower every day for years and stared at the horizon in the hope of seeing her beloved husband sailing back to her. But what *is* fact is that in her husband's absence she became the first and only female governor of Cuba.

The fortress now serves as a naval museum that is filled with rescued treasures from sunken ships. The showstopper is a replica of the famous Spanish warship *Santísima Trinidad*, the heaviest armed ship at the time; built in Havana, the imposing four-deck ship was sunk by the English during the Battle of Trafalgar offshore from Cádiz, Spain in 1805. [O'Reilly and Tacón]

The Kapok Tree

70 **El Templete** (The Temple) was built in 1828 to commemorate the first mass and the first city council meeting that saw the foundation of the town of San Cristóbal de La Habana (Havana) on November 16, 1519. The original ceremony allegedly took place on that exact spot in the shade of a giant, leafy kapok tree (*ceiba*, in Spanish). I LOVE that the kapok tree is still standing there nearly 500 years later—after 13 replantings that is!

The ceremony was immortalized by painter Jean Baptiste Vermay, the first director of the Escuela Nacional de Arte (National School of Arts), whose paintings adorn the interior of the Greco-Roman temple.

Every November 16, thousands of *habaneros* and tourists from around the world line up (sometimes several blocks long) to perform a ritual: They walk around the tree three times touching it with an outstretched arm and make three wishes with the hope that the *orishas* will grant their requests. To see if this really works, you will have to come to Havana and see for yourself! [northeast side of Plaza de Armas]

Old-World Charm

71 A palatial 18th-century home with singular archways and ornate balconies, and transformed into a hotel in 1867, this location has seen its share of counts, governors, traveling artists and musicians.

Wander through the grand lobby of the **Hotel Santa Isabel** with the colonial blue ceiling overhead, past the velvet sofas and fascinating artworks, before sitting down to a refreshing drink in its lush and light-filled atrium with a wall of fame of previous guests, like Jack Nicholson and Jimmy Carter. It really does feel like you have stepped back in time. But what I love most is the rooftop vibe and view. To one side is Plaza de Armas; Havana Bay is on the other. And while enjoying the view, there is live music, salsa dancing, and did I mention cocktails? Swirling in the sunshine is euphoric. [Baratillo 9, btw Obispo and Narciso López]

ÁRBOL DE LUZ by RAFAEL VILLARES (Tree of Light)

Havana's Preeminent Literary Hotel

72 Ernest Hemingway lived in room 511 of **Hotel Ambos Mundos** between 1932 and 1939, making it his first residence in Havana before moving with his wife Martha Gellhorn to Finca Vigía (Reason #276), their country home in San Francisco de Paula on the outskirts of the city. His hotel room is now a museum with all the same furnishings, including his single bed, his typewriter, reading glasses and fishing rods. This is where he wrote *For Whom the Bell Tolls*, while enjoying the view of the Havana harbor, where he docked his fishing boat *Pilar*. You can just show up at room 511 and take a five minute tour, which plunges you into the life of the American writer Cubans call their own. The hotel has long attracted writers and actors from around the globe.

The rooftop terrace offers a great view of Habana Vieja. It's a nice place to enjoy a piña colada and some sun.

The imposing lobby is lined with black-and-white photographs of Hemingway. The bar or loungy sofas—the perfect spot for an espresso—is where you are treated to masterful music on the grand piano. [Obispo 153, btw Mercaderes and San Ignacio]

Get Your Guayabera On!

73 If you want to look the part while in Havana, you need to get yourself a guayabera. This traditional Cuban shirt—typically made of linen or cotton—is a loose-fitting button down with four pockets and pressed pleats. A great place to buy one is the state-run shop **El Quitrín** on Obispo, near San Ignacio.

They have long and short-sleeved cuts, dresses and adorable versions for kids that are impossible to resist. [Obispo 163, btw Mercaderes and San Ignacio]

You Have Arrived

74 Touristy, but full of locals, **Café París** is the one ember that never went out—even during the *periodo especial*. A state-owned institution on the corner of Obispo and San Ignacio, this restaurant-bar has one of the best settings in Havana. It has typical Cuban fare and its stellar lineup of terrifically energetic Cuban bands make it an ideal place to be any time of day. When you walk by and hear the enveloping rhythms of the traditional *son cubano* emanating from the open doors, you know you are in Havana. Take a look at the caricature of El Caballero de París (Reason #42) and the emblematic neon sign over the bar. [San Ignacio 22, corner Obispo]

Dress the part We are in a civilized European-influenced city in the Caribbean. Cubans dress up at night. Men wear long pants and shirts; women are elegant. Havana is not a beach resort.

Mural by @abstrk and @ mr_myl

Havana Pizza

75 "Hole-in-the-wall" pizza, served through a small window of a house or an entranceway can be found throughout the city. I've been enjoying these homemade pizzas since my first visit to Havana in 1989. Tomato sauce, cheese and dough never tasted so good!

If you peek inside you can see a mini assembly line of cooks rolling out pizza dough, slathering on tomato sauce, sprinkling cheese and then tossing the individual-sized pizzas into small ovens. The whole process takes about five minutes per pizza. They always come out piping hot with soft fluffy crust and gooey cheese. Walking around the city while polishing off your pizza—folded in half is the Cuban way—is a quintessential Havana experience. When I get a craving, one of my favorite spots is **Cafetería El Milagro**. While it's not the finest pizza in the world, there is something about the texture, the freshness that makes this pizza like no other! [Obispo, btw Cuba and San Ignacio]

Aristocratic Architecture

76 Greeting you with a graceful nude sculpture in the entrance hall, the **Hotel Florida** is a classic Old Havana aristocratic home that was converted into a grand hotel, catering to well-heeled American and European guests. Walk in through impossibly tall doors and see the grandiose open courtyard with sumptuous wicker furniture and lush tropical plants. Colonial glory aside, my favorite spot is the **Maragato Piano Bar**, one of the best salsa scenes in town. Arrive early to beat the dance-savvy crowd to a seat—though you won't likely be sitting for long! This intimate venue gets moving quickly when some of the best dancers in the city arrive, including salsa teachers who bring their students here to put their lessons to the test. [Obispo, btw Cuba and Aguiar]

Medicinal Time Capsule

77 **Droguería Johnson** is a fairy-tale pharmacy founded in 1886 by Dr. Manuel Serafín Johnson Larralde and his son Teodoro Agustin Johnson Anglada. It is still in operation today. It was nationalized after the revolution and it is now part pharmacy, part museum. The American engineering firm that specialized in metal structures, Purdy and Henderson, gets acclaim for this formidable building. The immaculate white porcelain jars lining the walls are all empty, but they give a glimpse into a long-ago glory, as does the beautiful carved wood casing and the golden moldings deserving of a church cupola. Reproductions of the jars are for sale. The few pharmaceutical goods available for purchase from a display case on the counter are eclipsed by this must-see medicinal mecca. [Obispo 260, corner Aguiar]

Books Galore

78 The 1959 Cuban Revolution assured that everyone had access to education and that also implied access to inexpensive books—Cubans are huge readers. As José Martí said: "*Ser culto para ser libre*" (Be educated to be free).

Fayad Jamis Bookstore has books in Spanish and English, most of which you can still purchase at subsidized prices, as well as maps of Havana for travelers. [Obispo, corner Aguiar]

79A

Golden Rain on Obispo

79 **La Lluvia del Oro** (A) is a happening state-run café on Calle Obispo that has been around since the 1930s. It is unpretentious with chunky wooden square tables and a few black-and-white photos scattered on the side wall. I love the feel of the spacious interior with huge open windows, the generously sized old-world bar and the professionalism of the waiters in white shirts and black vests. The last time I zipped in for a coffee, an unbelievable band with deep soulful voices left me with shivers. When the singers started swirling in sync, I was riveted. I was photographing and filming at the same time for future salsa self-tutoring. The band invited the nearest table to get up and follow suit and soon the entire bar was lit. [Obispo 316, corner Habana]

Around the corner is **Fajoma** (B), a wonderful find, three stories high with treats on each floor. One level up is a handsome cigar lounge with the most unprecedented humidor hidden inside a secret door of an arresting wooden wall shaped like the Cuban flag. Head to the cozy rooftop terrace for pineapple pork and a peanut colada. Live music three times a week on ground, mezzanine and terrace! Fajoma is derived from the names of triplets (Fadi, Joseph and Maria) of a Cuba devotee and contributor to the establishment. [Compostela 313, btw Obispo and Obra Pía; +535 249 6342]

Bring gifts Chocolate, candies, gum, pens, perfume, soap, shampoo, cream, clothing and over-the-counter medications. Pack whatever you can in your bag and you will find someone to give it to.

on lo imposible .

Graffiti by diseck & holow

A-to-Z Souvenir Spree

81 **Feria de Obispo** is an artisan market right on Calle Obispo that is the perfect place to get gifts on the go: leather wallets, paintings, wooden statuettes, key chains, jewelry, hats. Dozens of vendors are all elbow-to-elbow at tiny kiosks crammed with their crafts. A fun gift is a "beer-can camera," a small souvenir camera that has been fashioned out of a can of Cristal or Bucanero, two local brews. Sold in many souvenir shops in Old Havana, these adorable and clever gadgets are pure Cuban inventiveness at work. You can actually press the shutter button (a piece of metal) and out through the "lens" comes a spring-loaded image of a clown or silly face. [Obispo 411, btw Aguacate and Compostela]

Mojito to Measure

80 Sometimes a place just feels right the moment you walk in. From the outside, **La Dichosa** looks like one of many small musical bars on Calle Obispo but the vibe is so welcoming, you can't help but pop in for a cold one—and the ultra-friendly staff will keep you there for more.

When a shortage of glassware forced them to become resourceful, they didn't disappoint. Beer mugs were called into action for the newly christened "Big Mojito," now with star billing on the sandwich board beckoning you in. You need go no further than this unpretentious corner hot spot for urban authentic. [Obispo, corner Compostela]

82A

At nearby **Sibarita** (B) [O'Reilly 528, btw Bernaza and Villegas; +535 267 0512], meaning "epicurean," the music never stops and the scintillating staff are most likely to dance a drink to your banquette. This festive rooftop bar is bursting with a frenzy of colorful street art, including a full wall mural by Luis Casas (aka Mr. MYL), a pioneer of the Cuban graffiti and urban art movement in Havana, plus neon lights and a luxuriant garden with cute palm trees. The Sibarazo and Sexy Mojito are just two of their signature cocktails that you can enjoy with *bolas de macabi* (balls of locally caught bonefish) and cheese-and-basil empanadas.

Daiquiris, Dancing and Dining

82 **El Floridita** (A) [Obispo 557, corner Monserrate] is one of Havana's most famous attractions and it is always teeming with tourists. The pink exterior is emblematic, but wait until you get inside and see the monumental red bar, complete with a huge painting of the Havana harbor.

Professional waiters in red jackets or aprons, with crisp white shirts and red ties, blend and pour their signature ice-cold daiquiris in a dazzling show. At the far-left corner of the bar sits a life-size bronze statue of Ernest Hemingway, seemingly ready to converse, but instead resigned to endless selfies.

There is always a first-rate band playing near the front entrance, often with a beautiful lead singer—with an expansive smile—dancing and playing maracas. It's impossible not to dance along. Or just feast on the spectacle and crispy chips that come with your drink.

82B

A Scene from Graham Greene

83

Spanish immigrant José Abeal y Otero opened his bar in 1917 in what was a grocery store in Old Havana. During the Prohibition era in the United States (1920 to 1933), **Sloppy Joe's** became "cocktail central" in Havana. After being closed for nearly 50 years, this historic institution was restored by the Office of the City Historian (Reason #65); each detail was refabricated with the help of period photos and relics donated both in Cuba and abroad.

You can find the same *ropa vieja* sandwiches (Sloppy Joes with pulled pork) that were served in its heyday and their signature cocktail—a blend of brandy, port, Cointreau and pineapple juice served in a martini glass, which I will forego for one of their mojitos made with Santiago de Cuba rum.

A scene from the 1959 movie *Our Man in Havana* was shot here. The film, starring Alec Guinness, was based on the novel by British author Graham Greene, one of Sloppy Joe's former patrons. The black-and-white movie runs on a loop on their TV screens.

Check out the nearly 60-foot (18-meter) mahogany bar and vintage photos from the 1930s. [Zulueta 252, btw Ánimas and Virtudes]

Havana's Art Deco Mecca

84

The most complete and beautiful example of art deco in Havana, the **Edificio Bacardí** is one of my favorite buildings in the city. Who doesn't love this arresting masterpiece? Built in 1930 by the Bacardí Rum family, it was the city's first "skyscraper" and continues to be one of the most opulent and evocative buildings in the capital.

Students of architecture and interior design spend hours here in awe admiring every last detail: geometric elements; sumptuous polished marble interior; red Bavarian granite exterior; enameled terracotta panels of naked nymphs by American artist Maxfield Parrish; and the iconic Bacardí bat symbol, the brainchild of one of the Bacardí wives, that crowns the roof.

While access to the 12-story building is confined to the main lobby, and the sleek secretive second floor café-bar, go. It is an absolute must. [Monserrate 261, corner San Juan de Dios]

National Treasure Troves

85

The most comprehensive collection of Cuban art in the world can be found at the **Museo Nacional de Bellas Artes**. Spread out over two sites, **Centro Asturiano** (A) [San Rafael, btw Zulueta and Monserrate] focuses on international art, while the **Edifício de Arte Cubano** (B) [Trocadero, btw Zulueta and Monserrate] is devoted to Cuban art. Cruise through diverse and intriguing works from 17th-century colonial Cuban artists to 1960s pop to the present, all arranged chronologically. Don't miss the remarkable works of Guillermo Collazo, Flavio Garciandía, Juan Francisco Elso Padilla, Eduardo Ponjuán, José Bedia, René Portocarrero, Wifredo Lam, Manuel Mendive Hoyo (Reason #223), and Esterio Segura (Reason #270), among other Cuban shining stars.

86A

Five-Star Grandeur

86

Havana's first genuine five-star hotel post-revolution, the **Gran Hotel Manzana Kempinski La Habana** (A) opened for business in 2017 with 246 rooms and suites, a spa with steam rooms, Jacuzzis and Finnish saunas, three restaurants, a rooftop terrace with infinity pool, a tobacco lounge and a world-class gym. To top it off, there is also art by contemporary Cuban artists, including Omara López Segrera, Victor Mora, Alberto Flores and custom-made images for every floor by Claudia Corrales (Reason #285), the granddaughter of Raúl Corrales, one of Fidel Castro's personal photographers.

Housed in the immaculately restored 19th-century Manzana de Gómez building, originally a commercial center with luxury stores, the hotel keeps the shopping tradition alive with high-end brand-name boutiques in the ground floor mall.

Surrounded by the Paseo del Prado, Gran Teatro, El Capitolio, Parque Central, Museo de Bellas Artes and El Floridita, the Kempinski is a jewel in the crown of this gorgeous city. [Calle San Rafael, btw Monserrate and Zulueta; +537 869 9104]

Walk to their new establishment **Gran Hotel Bristol La Habana** (B) just a few blocks away. Hands down the best rooftop view of the Capitolio (Reason #111) [Teniente Rey, btw Zulueta and Monserrate; +537 823 2625]

86A

85

87 A

Vintage and Brand-New Accommodations on the Prado

87

Built in the early 1900s, the marvelous **Hotel Sevilla** (A), [Trocadero 155, btw Paseo del Prado and Zulueta; +537 860 8560] run by Meliã, stands apart with its neo-Moorish mesmerizing facade. Once the Sevilla Biltmore and a major Mafia hangout, its past patrons include underworld figures like Lucky Luciano, Meyer Lansky and Al Capone, whose photo hangs in the front lobby. It is a location in Graham Greene's novel *Our Man in Havana*, where the protagonist joins the British Secret Intelligence Service.

New 5-star hotels have mushroomed along the Prado. **The Grand Packard** (B) by Iberostar [Prado, btw Cárcel and Genios; +537 823 2100] is a stylish blend of old and new, built upon the original 100-year-old hotel, adding a sleek, square structure equipped with a dramatic view of the entrance to the harbor beyond the infinity pool. Traveling by helicopter? You can land on the roof of Royalton's **Paseo del Prado** (C)

[Prado, corner Malecón; +537 823 2400], a new building with nine floors of rooms culminating in a neverbeforeseen rooftop vista of the harbor. Or envision a stay at Royalton's boutique hotel **Mystique Regis Habana** (D) for adults only [Prado, corner Colón; +537 886 4501].

87 D

88 A

Havana's Hall of Mirrors

88

Built in the early 20th century as the new seat for the Government of Havana Province, the building that now houses the **Museo de la Revolución** (A) was so spectacular that the governor's wife convinced her husband to take it over and make it their home; it became, however, the Presidential Palace—up until the end of Fulgencio Batista's presidency in 1959. It would be later taken over by the revolutionary government. In 1974, it became a museum dedicated to the Cuban Revolution. Here, you can see bullet holes in the main stairway from a failed assassination attempt on President Batista; bloodstained soldiers' uniforms; remarkable photographs of Fidel Castro, Che Guevara, Camilo Cienfuegos, Celia Sánchez and other revolutionary leaders in different stages of combat; as well as exhibits dedicated to El Che (Guevara) and the 1953 Moncada attack.

As spectacular as the exhibits are, the building itself is something to behold with its fabulous interior decor by Tiffany of New York and its stunning Salón de los Espejos (Hall of Mirrors), which was modeled after the eponymous gallery at the Palace of Versailles.

Pay a visit to the statue of José Martí on horseback in front of the museum depicting the moment he was shot.

Don't miss the **Granma** (B), the yacht displayed in a huge glass box behind the museum. Fidel, Raúl, Che and their fellow revolutionaries sailed the craft from Mexico to Cuba in 1956 in one of their first attempts at toppling the government. [Refugio 1, btw Zulueta and Monserrate]

90

Find It and Love It

89

Upstairs in a colonial house, eclectic decor lines the walls through this labyrinth-like restaurant with a rooftop terrace that is ready to wow. You feel like you have really lucked out when you step outside.

Ivan Chef Justo (A) [Aguacate 9, corner Chacón; +535 258 3627] is one of the primo *paladares* in the city with its farm-sourced produce and fresh sea bounty that shouts Cuba. Depending on what's available that day, you might score *caldereta de pescado* (fish stew), tuna tartare, hand-rolled pasta, baby-eel salad, suckling pig or seafood paella. The much-heralded kitchen virtuosos Ivan and Justo have amassed such a huge following that they opened another restaurant around the corner. **Al Carbón** (B) [Chacón, corner Aguacate] creates new takes on traditional Cuban favorites and, as its name suggests, there is a lot of grilling going on.

89 B

Harleys and Tapas

90

You could easily mistake **Chacón 162** for a Madrid or Rome eatery because the outdoor terrace has such a European vibe to it. The restaurant's unique facade juts out in a triangle toward Chacón and Compostela streets, further enhancing its romantic appeal.

This lively tapas bar's food rivals its elaborate cocktails overflowing with rum, fruit and garnishes.

It also happens to be the unofficial headquarters of motorcycle enthusiasts known as "Cuban Harlistas." In fact, Ernesto Guevara (Che's son) is one of the restaurant's regulars and he donated the motorcycle that is hanging on the wall behind the bar. Motorcycle tours with Ernesto (La Poderosa Tours) can be booked at lapoderosatours.com.

Motorcycle buffs, and everyone else, will feel right at home at the friendly neighborhood clubhouse. [Chacón 162, corner Compostela; +537 860 1386]

Restaurant Central

91

The intersection of Habana, Cuarteles and Espada streets come together in a five-pointed star. At the junction is **5 Esquinas** (A) (Five Corners) **Trattoria** [Habana 104, corner Cuarteles; +537 860 6295] a modern Italian eatery with authentic wood-fired pizzas, home-made pasta, gnocci and risotto. I love to eat outdoors on tables that are laid out on cobblestones between buildings. The soft romantic lighting is so perfect that you feel like you are on a movie set.

Hang out at **Habana 5** (B), the rooftop restaurant bar with the most heart-stirring view of the Morro Castle (Reason #280). Specializing in seafood and tropical inspired cocktails, it is also a five-room boutique hotel. Try the most flavorful albacore tuna tartare, grouper tiradito and supreme daiquiris. [Habana 5, btw Peña Pobre and Bélgica; +535 551 9987]

The Community Leader Who Cuts It

92 Which city in the world has a Hairdressers' Alley? Havana, of course! The brainchild of legendary coiffeur Gilberto "**Papito**" Valladares—became a reality when a stretch of Calle Aguiar, one of Havana's worst roads, was turned into a beautiful 330-foot (100-meter) pedestrian paradise, benefitting the whole community. Everyone in the alley saw their incomes rise and their living standards improve. The **Callejón de los Peluqueros** is now home to restaurants and a nonprofit hairdressing school where you can just walk in to get a haircut. [+535 197 2996] Papito's **Arte Corte** hair salon doubles as the **Casa Museo de la Barbería**, a barbershop museum filled with antique scissors, brushes, mirrors,and other old relics from Papito's personal collection. [For a museum tour email proyectoartecorte@gmail.com]

Papito maintains his passion about his community projects and believes that life is about giving back to the people. He spoke with Barack Obama at an entrepreneurship event in Havana in March 2016. The president said to him: "Papito, I know that my barber is very important to me. And Michelle's hairdresser... If she had to choose between me and her hairdresser, I don't know, it would be a close call! And so congratulations on not only starting your business, but also seeing it as a social enterprise that can help to contribute to the well-being of the community as a whole."

Papito created the **Monument to Barbers and Hairdressers**, a 9-foot (3-meter) high statue of a pair of scissors onto which he welded shears donated by his coiffing colleagues worldwide.

With all his accolades, I couldn't believe it was actually possible to get an appointment with him. But I did, on a 100-year-old barber's chair, and had a soulful conversation to boot.

Within view of the monument, Bistro **La Bearnesa** [Callejón de los Peluqueros (Aguiar) 18, btw Pena Pobre and Avenida de las Misiones; +535 293 6475] serves Lobster in Coffee Sauce, created accidentally when Chef Gilberto Smith spilled espresso on the lobster he was preparing for French President François Mitterrand.

Open in 2016 by carpenter, upholsterer and vintage aficionado Alan Castro Granda, **ChaChaChá** (B) reverberates with good vibes. This Old Havana hot spot has live music every day of the week, is open from lunch 'til late and serves luscious ceviche, as well as funghi and truffle risottos. Sit at the bar for a mesmerizing mixology show by no-nonsense bartenders. [Monserrate 159, btw Tejadillo and Chacón; +535 196 8888]

Effortlessly Cool, Authentically Cuban

93 The vibe! The design! The staff! The food! Wedged in a narrow 18th-century lane lined with restaurants is **Antojos** (A). Just when you think the shaded tables on cobblestone is the dreamiest setting...wait until you go inside. Antojos, "cravings" in Spanish, will satisfy them all, including your yearning for fun and music.

Greeted by exuberant staff who dazzle with their rhythm and moves, all while offering 5-star service, the eclectic space is a sensory banquet. You are surrounded by classic neon signage emblematic of 1930s Havana, a 1950s Sputnik chandelier, a zebra motif banquette and we haven't even gotten to the food. The menu features nearly every traditional Cuban dish, from starters like chicken croquettes and fish fingers, to chicken fricassée and BBQ dishes that taste as though they were made by *guajiros* over a charcoal pit in the 19th century Cuban countryside. The ribs are considered the city's best.

Order a freshly squeezed lemonade or a "Mary Pickford," a Prohibition-Era cocktail made of white rum, fresh pineapple juice and grenadine by the bubbly bartender who got me off my seat to rumba. Desserts of the day are right out of an *abuela*'s (grandma's) kitchen. [Callejón Espada, btw Cuarteles and Chacón; +535 282 4907]

Two Hip Havens

94 Just off frenzied Calle Obispo, the main drag where tourists abound and Cubans hustle in their day to day, lays a clandestine oasis. **Revolution Boutique Hotel** (A) [Habana 156 #8, btw Obispo and Obra Pía; +537 867 4309], hidden down the teal-blue corridor of an aging residential building and through a regular apartment door, is a multiroom sanctuary, ingenuously designed to refit the space with an elevated interior courtyard infusing light and greenery for a glorious feel. Its little sister hotel is **Art Boutique Habana** (B), with a small art gallery, in the middle of restaurant central. [Habana 155, btw Chacón and Tejadillo; +537 862 7703]

Havana Masala

95 Cuba's first gourmet Indian restaurant, **Buena Vista Curry Club** (shoutout for the name!), was created by multifaceted businessperson Paramjit Chhatwal and young budding Cuban entrepreneur Aida Ivis Fernández. They have assuaged the epicurian needs and curiosity of locals and tourists alike. They brought spices and seasonings not commonly found in Cuba to the table, and use coal-fired tandoor ovens that impart an exquisite flavor, to create mouthwatering dishes—chicken tikka masala, fish curry and tikka sourced direct from local fishermen and the best naan I can remember. Head chef Bimal Kishor, formally trained in the culinary arts in North India, was scooped up from none other than the Lalit Hotel of New Delhi! Chhatwal has lived and worked in Havana for decades and had long wanted to bring his home country's cuisine to Old Havana; and he has done so with panache. You are sure to drink excellent wine here, as Chhatwal is also a wine and cigar connoisseur and he has made sure to stock BVCC's wine cellar with refined old-world wines.

Apart from satisfying my Indian food cravings, I love coming here for the ambiance of the exquisite dining room and, believe it or not, BVCC has jazz musicians performing nightly.

Spot the chic and discreet neon sign on the corner of the building and you have arrived. [Tejadillo 24, corner Cuba; +535 975 7791]

Contemporary, Compassionate, Contemplative Art

96 My good friend and exceptional contemporary artist Nelson Ramirez de Arellano is director of **Centro de Arte Contemporáneo Wifredo Lam**, named in honor of Cuba's beloved modernist artist renowned for cubist and surrealist works that reclaim African identity. The art center was founded in 1983 with the mission of researching and promoting contemporary visual art from Africa, the Middle East, Asia, Latin America and the Caribbean, and to investigate and promote the life's work of Wilfredo Lam. Housed in a 1700s structure with an expansive indoor courtyard framed by colonnades, the center also hosts the Havana Biennial, the largest visual arts event in Cuba, showcasing artists worldwide in mesmerizing installations across the city. [San Ignacio 22, corner Empedrado; +537 861 2096]

Latin America's Beloved Novelist

98

Museo Alejo Carpentier, just a few steps from La Bodeguita del Medio (Reason #97), pays tribute to the life of Alejo Carpentier, one of Cuba's most important 20th-century authors. The staff is welcoming, as is the pretty courtyard beckoning you to enter. Here, you can learn about the life of this fascinating novelist, playwright, musicologist and social activist who influenced a whole generation of Latin American writers, including Leonardo Padura (Reason #272) and Gabriel García Márquez.

Carpentier's family moved to Havana in 1905 when he was an infant. Despite being born in Switzerland to French parents, Carpentier considered himself a Cuban; he deeply loved his adoptive homeland—and Cuba loved him back. [Empedrado 215, btw Cuba and San Ignacio]

Home of the Mojito

97

The hub for mojitos and genuine Cuban grub since 1942, Havana's most renowned watering hole is a beloved spot despite being a major tourist destination. Like an assembly line, glasses are lined up on the bar, unremittingly filled by a guayabera-wearing bartender with Havana Club rum, soda, cane sugar, Angostura bitters and well-crushed mint. *Salud*!

Sit at the bar and hear a trio wholeheartedly sing "Comandante Che Guevara," and for the full effect, look up to see a photo of Fidel Castro and Ernest Hemingway shaking hands, a testament to their sole encounter. Notables who have frequented **La Bodeguita del Medio** are Pablo Neruda, Chilean President Salvador Allende, Marlene Dietrich and Gabriel García Márquez. Sign your name on the wall...if you can find a spot. [Empedrado 207, btw Cuba and San Ignacio]

18th-Century Beauty

99 When you are in **Plaza de la Catedral** [San Ignacio and Empedrado] you feel as though time has stood still as this old town square looks pretty much exactly the same as when it was founded. One of Old Havana's five squares, there is no denying its beauty. Anchored by the jaw-dropping Catedral de la Habana at the northern edge of the square, and surrounded by 18th-century baroque mansions, it is hard to believe that this was once swampland; one of the original monikers of the square was Plaza de la Ciénaga (Swamp Square).

The plaza is often the site of important outdoor concerts, exhibits and celebrations organized by the Office of the City Historian, like yours truly's first Havana photo exhibit hung between the arches of the **Palacio del Conde Lombillo** in celebration of the city's 500th anniversary in 2019, and concerts organized by Instituto de la Música, like the unbelievable New Year's Eve bash hosted by the state-owned El Patio restaurant on its western edge. On December 31, the eve of the anniversary of the Cuban Revolution, the entire plaza is transformed into an elegant outdoor dining room.

Also in the plaza is ever-so-chic and centrally located **INNSiDE Habana Catedral**, a boutique hotel run by Meliã. [Empedrado 113, btw Mercaderes and Tacón; +537 886 4700]

Divine Cuban Comfort Cuisine

100 **Paladar Doña Eutimia**, a Havana classic, is tucked away at the end of el Callejón del Chorro near Plaza de la Catedral. The staff serves up Cuban favorites such as *croquetas de Leticia, ropa vieja, pollo grillé* and *pescado grillé* with their homemade salsa—garlic, olive oil and Cuban rum, all served with delicious black beans, rice and fried plantains. They make a pro mojito frappé; it is like a Slush Puppie for adults. The restaurant's name is a tribute to Eutimia, a much-loved woman who lived nearby and used to cook for the artists working at the Taller Experimental de Gráfica (Reason #103) adjacent to the restaurant.

The inside of the *paladar* is intimate, with dark carved wood, eclectic Cuban art and comfortable wicker furniture. Out front is a romantically lit terrace for alfresco dining, with a live band serenading. This used to be the only restaurant down the tiny alley, but now there is an entire hive of them and it's abuzz every night of the week. [Callejón del Chorro 60-C; +535 328 4713]

102A

Wine on The Prado

102 **Del Prado** (A) [Prado 158, btw Refugios and Colón; +535 036 1722] is a gourmet Mediterranean-inspired restaurant, opened in 2023, that sources food from its own farm, **Finca Vista Hermosa** (Reason #291), and boasts the most exclusive Italian wine list in the city. Pair a piadina, farm-fresh cheeses or vegetarian risotto with a refreshing juice or glass of Petite Arvine from Valle d'Aosta served by expert sommeliers. Set in a neoclassical house with a sky-high ceiling, antique colonial floor tiles and wood-beam mezzanines, you can also just pop in for a stellar espresso and croissant.

Extend your wine tasting repertoire at nearby **PlanH** (B), a sleek wine bar that takes pride in its cellar, teachings and decor. It even serves breakfast! [Prado 308, btw Ánimas and Virtudes; +537 861 6212]

Conceptual Cafés

101 **Esto no es un Café** (A) pays tribute to artists who have left their mark on history with dishes such as Broodthaers's Casserole, Lam's Third World, Pollock's Chicken, and Duchamp's Fountain to name a few. [Callejón del Chorro 58A; +537 801 3109]

Fonda Al Pirata (B) [San Ignacio 76, btw O'Reilly and Callejón del Chorro; +535 343 7812] is one of the first restaurants in Havana to offer a vegan menu, including smoothies, natural fruit juices and an invigorating ginger-carrot power shot. Just half a block from Plaza de la Catedral, this pirate-themed restaurant with a fantastic playlist and outdoor tables on the cobblestone street is a favorite spot for both locals and visitors looking for fresh, healthy food and drink. Breakfast is also served daily.

101B

Historic Canadian Bank Buildings

104

During one of my early trips to Havana, I was surprised to run across not just one, but two Canadian bank facades in Old Havana. Standing proud in all of their neoclassical grandeur, both the **Royal Bank of Canada** and **Bank of Nova Scotia** buildings seem almost identical to some of the historic branches in Old Montreal or downtown Toronto.

The Royal Bank at one time had as many as 65 branches in Cuba. In 1960 all foreign banks—except the Royal Bank and Bank of Nova Scotia—were nationalized but even they ultimately found that they could not compete with Che Guevara's Banco Nacional de Cuba and ended up selling their interests to the central bank.

I remember walking into the opulent Royal Bank building in 2009 while filming a documentary in Havana and I was surprised to find it completely hollow and used as a motorcycle garage. It has since been turned into office space.

Nevertheless, the bank names etched in stone are a reminder of the longstanding relationship between Canada and Cuba. [Royal Bank of Canada building: Aguiar 367, corner Obra Pía; Bank of Nova Scotia building: corner O'Reilly and Cuba]

The Cooperative Print Shop

103

The **Taller Experimental de Gráfica (TEG)** (A)was formed in 1962 when The Lithographic Company of Cuba and all its early 20th-century equipment was about to be scrapped. The saviors? A group of artists, including Cuban muralist Orlando Suárez and Chilean painter José Venturelli, who appealed to fellow countryman and poet Pablo Neruda, who convinced then—Cuban Minister of Industry Che Guevara to save the printmaking equipment and engraving stones. The TEG was created to use this equipment for artistic purposes, extending the tradition of Cuban printmaking dating from the 18th century. It turns out some of the most significant works of graphic art in the city.

Peek into the expansive ground-floor studio, then head upstairs where you can purchase original prints in the Galería del Grabado. [Callejón del Chorro]

Experimental Gallery (B) [Amargura 321, corner Aguacate] is an art gallery and souvenir shop run as a cooperative by local artists where it's easy to find something that is hard to resist.

La Ubre (C) [Tejadillo 108, btw Habana and Aguiar] is a small art studio founded by contemporary artists Michel Moro and Ramiro Zardoyas where all drawings, engravings and paintings are created by them.

105 B

Havana's Hip Hangouts

105 The grand central of ceviche and creative cocktails, **O'Reilly 304** (A) [O'Reilly 304, btw Habana and Aguiar; +537 863 0206] has long been the hottest spot on the Havana foodie scene. Chef and artist José Carlos and his photographer brother Julio are owners; they have created an epicurean mecca that you want to keep going back to because they have it all: outstanding staff, world-class food and exquisite drinks.

Everything is fresh: tacos filled with fish, pork or chicken, crisp lettuce, tomatoes, herbs; dreamy ceviche with white fish, onions, lime, garlic, white beans, coriander, chili; crunchy risotto croquettes; fried plantain with caviar!

The resto-bar became so popular that the brothers opened up a place across the street with the whimsical name **El del Frente** (B) (The One in Front) [O'Reilly 303, btw Habana and Aguiar; +535 322 7901]. Now it's hard to tell which is more popular.

El del Frente is stunning, with a wooden bar, suspended lighting, immense French windows, a collection of local art, including a masterpiece by Mabel Poblet (Reason #148) and a hopping terrace lounge. The food is spectacular; try my favorite starter—*Tostón Pelotón*—fried plaintains with ceviche, the seared tuna, the grilled lobster or their signature tacos. As for cocktails, when in season, their passion fruit mojitos or daiquiris steal the show, as do their famous gin drinks that are so ornate—and potent—they will leave you speechless. Their Habana-Londres is a gin and tonic with cherries that is topped with blue curacao to acknowledge the colors of both national flags. The piña coladas also deserve special mention. And watching the top-notch bartenders make them is half the fun.

Jama (C) [Aguiar 261b, btw San Juan de Dios and O'Reilly; +535 297 0745] is more than just an Asian-inspired restaurant, it is a dining experience with open kitchen, hip decor and excellent music playlist. It is where exceptional food is prepared from local, seasonal organic produce; only seaweed for the nigiri is imported. The menu features an entire section of rolls, and the tataki is made from fresh tuna caught in Cuban waters, the piña coladas are monumental, and fresh fruit daiquiris and cucumber-infused gin and tonics are slam dunks. They have a hibachi table where the chef cooks as you watch—try the lobster. "Jama" is slang for "eat" in Spanish and you will eat, and you will love it.

Two artists proudly featured at the unbelievable **Alma** (C) store are María Paula, who has her papermaking workshop on site, and artist and illustrator Iris Fundora, who conducts workshops for adults and children. Alma's mission is to promote Cuban design and empower the shop's female group of artists and designers. [Tejadillo 116, btw Habana and Aguiar]

On the second floor in an urban area decorated by street murals, discover **Beyond Roots** (D). Inspired by Cuba's African heritage, you'll find clothing with tribal prints and jewelry: you can even get your hair done in a salon tucked in the back. [San Ignacio 657, btw Jesus María and Merced]

Hungry for fantastic espresso and pastries as you shop? Head to **Gao Habana** (E) (*gao* is Cuban slang for home) for flamingo cushion covers, colorful woven beach bags and clothing by owner Annalisa Gallina. [Compostela 114, btw Tejadillo and Empedrado]

Bring Home Something Unique

106

These distinctive Old Havana boutiques showcase the contemporary local design community where you can find singular high-end gifts and souvenirs.

Piscolabis (A) is the OG of the genre, the city's first edgy boutique with handcrafted decorative items, many cleverly transformed from vintage or recycled pieces. Look out for Jennifer Rico's contemporary eye-themed jewelry called Mirar Por Dentro (look within) reminding us that our power lies within. [San Ignacio 75, btw Callejón de Chorro and O'Reilly]

On a prime corner along Obispo, the jaw-dropping storefront **Matty Habana** (B) promotes an array of functional items, such as poppy-themed napkin holders by Lucia Zalbidea Muñoz and Mayelín Guevara's jewelry made from every material under the sun—from silver to Formica. Find postcards, clothing, furniture: they have it all. [Obispo, corner San Ignacio]

Las Factorías

107

Spaniard Concha Fontenla is an award-winning curator who has worked closely with the Office of the City Historian to produce two astonishing Old Havana galleries that are indisputable proof of her celebrated impact on the perpetually evolving Cuban art scene. **Factoría Habana** (A) [O'Reilly 308, btw Habana and Amagura], a vast retrofitted space that maintained its factory-like quality with towering ceilings and cast-iron columns, encourages the fusion of contemporary art and technology. Right next to the harbor, she has created **Factoría Diseño** (B) [Santa Clara 8, btw Oficios and Avenida del Puerto] featuring mid-20th century furniture, art, jewelry, handbags and a full coffee and cocktail bar. With a careful eye and relentless patience, Concha unearths some of the most beautiful pieces, some having taken years to restore, and displays them like museum artifacts, so that you don't even realize that everything is for sale.

107 A

A Walk in the Park

108

Parque Cervantes, also known by locals as Parque San Juan de Dios, is a leafy landscaped green reprieve from the densely populated narrow streets of Old Havana. Walking paths crisscross the park and intersect in the center at an imposing marble statue of Miguel de Cervantes, the great Spanish writer best known for his masterpiece *Don Quixote,* a must-read in school. The park was inaugurated in 1908 on the site of the former San Juan de Dios hospital. Even if you only have time to walk across it, the treed oasis provides a cool break from the Havana heat.

108

A Muse to Amuse

109 The name and decor of the restaurant-bar **El Antonia** (A) is inspired by a character thought up by owner Odette Patoja. She imagined a muse, an alter ego of sorts, who would inspire artists and bohemians. She then integrated the spirit of Antonia by placing a fantasy early 20th century bedroom right above the bar. When Odette's friend, writer Maité Hernández-Lorenzo, saw her creation, it inspired her to compose a short story in which the irresistibly charming Antonia, welcomes guests with her tempting allure, singing and dancing while they revel in smoking and drinking until the wee hours. The 'real' establishment presents choice musical shows, from jazz to opera to alternative rock. [Compostela 116, btw Tejadillo and Empedrado; +535 270 8047]

Around the corner is groove central, **La Casona del Son** (B), your dream locale for private or group dance lessons for all skill levels and styles...salsa, son, rumba, cha-cha-cha and more. [Emperdado 411, btw Aguacate and Compostela; +535 274 7709 (contact Dayana for appointments); info@lacasonadelson.com]

110 A

A Charismatic Dancer and Influential Woman

110 When she was just a little girl, Lizt Alfonso couldn't resist busting a move whenever she heard music, so at four years old her mother took her to see the National Ballet of Cuba perform Coppélia at the Grand Teatro (Reason #113). From that moment onward, she lost herself to dance.

Known for her inimitable charismatic dance style, Alfonso created **Lizt Alfonso Dance Cuba** (A) [Compostela 659, btw Luz and Acosta; +537 866 3680] at 23 years old. She has directed the dance company since its inception and performed until 1998. Lizt's numerous accolades include: appointed UNICEF Goodwill Ambassador in Cuba in 2011, named one of the world's 100 most influential women in 2018 by the BBC, and an International Spotlight Award for her exceptional contribution in the realms of education and social work presented by Michelle Obama at the White House. Her dance troupe performed at the Latin Grammy awards and in Enrique Iglesias's video *Bailando* featuring Cuban musicians Descemer Bueno and Gente de Zona—one of the most-viewed videos of all time.

To witness her unique fusion of flamenco, ballet and Afro-Cuban rhythms, try to catch a performance at the Teatro Martí (Reason #60) or tour the company's impressive headquarters in the Old Havana complex that she founded with the help of Eusebio Leal (Reason #65) or take dance lessons at **Malecón ART 255** (B), which opened in 2022. [Malecón 255, btw Blanco and Galiano; +537 866 0740]

CENTRO HABANA

This densely populated area with its raw feel is a bustling working-class neighborhood and a great place to get real with the *gente de a pie* (ordinary people).

This is where the Malecón begins, the city's most famous *paladar*, La Guarida, is located and the main hospital Los Hermanos Almeijeiras juts out as its only high-rise. One of the oldest Chinatowns (*Barrio Chino*) in Latin America is located here, as are Havana's main commercial streets, San Rafael and Neptuno, developed in the early 1900s.

National Pride

111

Located on the border of Old Havana and Centro Habana, the city's iconic landmark **El Capitolio Nacional** is Kilometer Zero for Cuba's national highway system. The 24-carat diamond under the dome marks the spot.

Walk up the resplendent steps of the Capitolio past sculptures symbolizing the mythic Guardians of Virtue and Work, and I guarantee that you will feel the immensity of it all. The magnificent interior is full of granite columns, marble floors and bronze doors. Look up to see the spectacular dome, and behold one of the largest indoor statues in the world, the 36-foot (11-meter) high gold-plated bronze *Statue of the Republic*.

Go to the main library—dedicated to José Martí—and don't miss the tremendous Tiffany chandeliers. Walk down the stunning Hall of Lost Steps, where the acoustics make for "silent footsteps." Once you are humbled by the splendor and magnitude, take a stroll and soak up the atmosphere in the surrounding French-designed gardens.

Built in 1929, this grandiose building was the former seat of the Cuban government, and since the revolution has housed the Cuban Academy of Sciences and the National Library of Science and Technology. After five years of a complete overhaul finishing in 2018, including gold-plating the cupola, it once again houses the government. [Paseo de Martí 513, btw San José and Dragones] Contact San Cristóbal Travel Agency for an exclusive visit and tour; +537 801 7442.

Piano Bar with Ragazonne

112

Walk into the bar that oozes French-inspired Havana from the 1920s: the 15-foot (4.5-meter) high ceiling with its imposing chandeliers; the dazzling bar; the baroque gold-leafed framed black-and-white photos; a jazzy, sexy atmosphere; the effortless style of the staff and the lighting that makes everything shine right.

Not to mention Gustavo Echevarría's (Reason #153) audacious art, blessed live music and a grand piano to boot! Enter **Michifú** through the regal velvet stage curtain and brace yourself for the elegant eclectic vibe. [Concordia 368, corner Escobar; +537 862 4869]

Gran Teatro

113 One of the ultimate things to do in Havana is to catch a show at the **Gran Teatro de La Habana Alicia Alonso**, named after Cuba's most famous prima ballerina; Alonso, who died in 2019, danced well into her 70s. I saw Alicia Alonso in the balcony watching a performance of *Giselle*, for which she is best remembered; at the end of the show the 96-year-old grande dame was escorted onto the stage by the ballerinas and curtseyed to an ecstatic crowd.

Be it the ballet, the opera, a musical or a play, tickets are sold at the theater's ticket counter right inside the front entrance. Shows are as awe-inspiring as the exquisite neobaroque building, which takes up the entire city block, and is gloriously lit at night. [Paseo de Martí 458, btw San José and San Rafael]

Revolutionary Lens

114 See the 1959 Cuban Revolution unfold through the lens of renowned photographer Raúl Corrales, who captured some of the most iconic photographs of Fidel Castro and Che Guevara as well as the spirit of the revolution. **Raúl Corrales Galería** is run by his granddaughter Claudia Corrales (Reason #285), also a gifted photographer. For an appointment call Claudia, +535 268 8684, or email: ccorralmesa@gmail.com. [O'Reilly 524, btw Monserrate and Villegas]

The Perfect Terrace to Take in the City

115

Havana's oldest hotel, the iconic **Hotel Inglaterra**, dates back to 1875 and sits right across from Parque Central (Reason #63). Cuban General Antonio Maceo (Reason #132) resided at the hotel for six months in 1890. Other notables have stayed there, including Winston Churchill who, in 1895, worked as a military reporter during the War for Cuban Independence.

The hotel has a majestic neoclassical facade and a spectacular outdoor terrace that is a prime place to take in the Havana spirit. Sit here with a cold drink, listen to live music and watch the steady crowds flurry past. It is also very LGTBQ+ friendly. [Paseo de Martí 416, corner San Rafael]

There is a helpful **excursion agency** in the lobby of Hotel Inglaterra where you can book day trips to places like Viñales, to visit the tobacco plantations, or to other cities, like Cienfuegos and Trinidad.

The Quintessential Stroll

116

Take a walk along the **Paseo del Prado** (simply known as el Prado), the eight-block-long promenade running north-south from the Malecón to Neptuno; it divides Centro Habana and Old Havana, and runs along the former fortification wall (Reason #54). It is a stunning marbled and tree-studded pedestrian esplanade originally designed in 1772 and remodeled in 1925 by French and Cuban landscape artists, who added the iconic bronze lions, marble benches and iron streetlamps. The bourgeoisie lived along Paseo del Prado before moving westward to Vedado and Miramar in the 20th century. The lone commercial remnant, now completely restored, is Casa Guerlain, the flagship Guerlain perfumery of the Americas, second only to the one in Paris, which opened in Havana in 1917 and reopened in 2016.

Paseo del Prado was the site of the famous 2016 Chanel fashion show; it turned the street into the grandest catwalk in the world.

On weekends you can buy paintings, photographs, hand-knit clothing and souvenirs at an arts and crafts market. I love the exuberant vibe when walking along this tree-canopied sanctuary with families wandering, teens rollerblading, kids playing soccer, men playing chess and life happening.

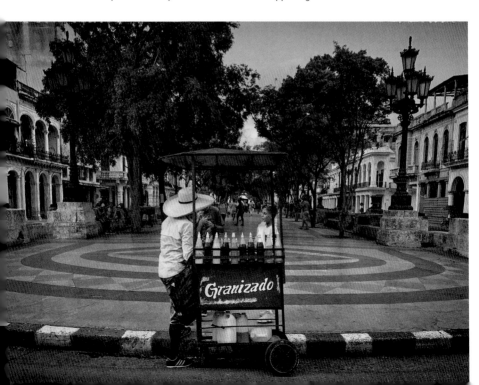

117

Satisfy Your Chinese Food Craving

118 The influx of Chinese laborers, who came to work on sugar plantations alongside enslaved Africans in the mid-19th century, led to Havana's ***Barrio Chino*** (Chinatown), one of the oldest and largest in Latin America. For the best Chinese food in the city, go to the Chinese gates (with the Capitolio behind you), walk down to the restaurant strip, and at the end to your left you'll find **Tien Tan** (Temple of Heaven). Using fresh ingredients, lots of garlic and sweet sauce, the Chinese and Cuban chefs turn out more than 100 delicious dishes. [Boulevard del Barrio Chino (Cuchillo) 17, btw Zanja and San Nicolás; +535 350 7947]

Tien Tan has a second location in Miramar. [Calle 46 #305, corner Avenida 3A]

The Gallery That Keeps Going

117 **Galleria Continua** opened in 2015 in Chinatown's Cine Águila de Oro, which used to screen kung fu and Japanese films. This is the ideal place to see high-end contemporary Cuban art. [Rayo 108, btw Zanja and Dragones]

118

Presidential Seal of Approval

119 Owner and chef **Carlos Cristóbal Márquez** has worked as a chef all over the world; in 2010 he opened **San Cristóbal** in his family home, adorning the early 20th-century mansion with eclectic decor from top to bottom.

Six presidents, including Barack Obama, have made a pilgrimage to this food mecca, as have countless celebrities, including Bon Jovi, Shania Twain and Sigourney Weaver.

Try the *pescado Florida* (fish with oranges), roast lamb, malanga purée or Carlos' self-proclaimed "best mashed potatoes" in the city. Because he is sensitive to the carbon footprint of his business Carlos specializes in Latin American wines, but has an ample cellar of very good wines from France, Germany, Portugal and South Africa. [San Rafael 469, btw Lealtad and Campanario; +535 339 4017]

Carlos' favorite place to go in Havana is La Punta (Reason #129), because it's romantic. "You sit there at midnight and if you look straight ahead you look down the Paseo del Prado or left and right down the Malecón—both are packed with people. But if you turn toward the entrance of the bay, there is no one. You can relax and talk to your friends or passersby."

When it comes to restaurants, Carlos likes to go to La Guarida (Reason #124) in his Centro Habana neighborhood and La Corte del Príncipe (Reason #246).

Hip Hotel with Local Impact

121 Founded by Andrés Levin, a Venezuela-born Grammy-winning music producer, and Canadian entrepreneur Chris Cornell along with his design team including savvy Jo-Anne Collar, **Tribe Caribe** is a concept-driven 11-room boutique hotel with 23 balconies, graced with giant murals by renowned Cuban painter Carlos Quintana. It houses an art gallery, café and **Manteca**, a sizzling rooftop bar-restaurant with unbeatable rhythms and 360-degree views of Havana accessed via an antique cage elevator. Set in Cayo Hueso, an emerging section of Centro Habana, the brand supports cultural projects in an effort to elevate the neighborhood and preserve the musical heritage so important to the community. A recording studio across the street makes this a destination for creatives. Among genuine experiences the hotel offers that plunge you headfirst into the real Havana is the bicycle taxi musical history tour of the 'hood to show where Juan Formell of Los Van Van and Omara Portuondo of Buena Vista Social Club were born. The experience also extends to eastern Havana's 1950s seaside town of Tarará (Reason #288), where Tribe Caribe organizes stays at its beach house getaway just 20 minutes away. [Aramburo #253, Corner Neptuno; +535 013 5030; tribecaribecayohueso.com]

Flavorful Fast Food

120 **La Juliana** is the place to go for a fast-food fix for delicious pizzas, hamburgers and their *tostones rellenos* (stuffed plantains), which are first class. Try one of their yummy milkshakes. [San Nicolás 210, corner Zanja]

Pizza-Perfect Sunset

122 You know you're at the right place once you step into the **Bleco** universe with its snazzy lounge feel, exquisite patio overlooking the Malecón, exceptional music, cutting edge mixology and the most famous pizza in Havana. The vibe here is one and of its own.

The restaurant was created in 2022 by contemporary dancer Lía Rodríguez and her dance producer husband Camilo Fernández Seguí. They wanted to turn what had become a weekly party for artists and other friends in their home into the chic but unpretentious, impeccably run restaurant it is today. Sunsets are sublime, and as the music picks up at dusk a sexy party ambiance reminiscent of Ibiza or Tulum sets in.

Their weekend brunches are legendary, with all-you-can-drink berry daiquiris, mimosas and slices of hot fresh pizza. My favorite is the vegetarian; a fan favorite is spicy chorizo. Just don't miss the truffle Parmesan fries! If you want to try their signature drink, ask for a Porn Star Martini. [Calle Marina 63, btw Vapor and Hornos; +535 013 9808]

Swedish-Cuban Vision

123 You gotta love Michel Miglis because he is such a nice guy and he opened one of the best restaurants in Havana, **Casa Miglis**. Everything is fresh and delicious: Swedish meatballs with mash potatoes, toast *skagen* (shrimp on toast), ceviche and the best gazpacho I've ever tasted...

They make daiquiris with real strawberries, a first-class Canchanchara and glorious mojitos. The funky decor, friendly staff, and supper dance extravaganza give the Miglis former home a perfect vibe. Book the epic Havana Queens dinner-dance show [reserve with Patrick +535 332 2415] and you might end up hitting the stage for the final dance frenzy, like I always do. [Lealtad 120, btw Animas and Lagunas; +535 282 7353]

The Essential Paladar

124

Part of the **La Guarida** restaurant experience is just getting there: walking up the battered grand marble staircase, past the Cuban flag painted on the crumbling wall, through the pristine white sheets hanging on clothespins and up another staircase past the headless statue of a broken goddess.

The czar of all *paladares*, La Guarida, founded by Enrique Núñez in 1996 in his family home, is legendary for many reasons: It was the setting for Cuba's most iconic film, *Fresa y Chocolate* (*Strawberry and Chocolate*), by Tomás Gutiérrez Alea and Juan Carlos Tabío; the food has always been top-notch and innovative (try the marlin tacos and Cuban ceviche—and my favorite dish, the sensational and visually stunning octopus carpaccio), and the restaurant is in constant evolution.

Along with its labyrinth of funky colorful rooms filled with fantastical sculptures, paintings and photographs, it has a gorgeous outdoor terrace as well as two rooftop bars.

I can never get enough of this place; it doesn't cease to amaze, and the vibe is always stellar. If you can only go to one restaurant on your Havana tour, this is it—but don't forget to book. [Concordia 418, btw Gervasio and Escobar; +535 414 7852]

Restaurateur Extraordinaire

Enrique Núñez grew up in Centro Habana, where he used to play baseball and soccer in the streets with the neighborhood kids. In 1993, his house was the setting for the film *Fresa y Chocolate*, the only Cuban film to have been nominated for an Academy Award. Following the film's success, fans from all over started showing up at the house in hope of seeing the Cuba portrayed in the film. But they were disappointed when it was found to be just a simple family home.

Around the same time, the Cuban government started giving out the first self-employment licenses; although his friends thought that he was crazy, Enrique decided to create a living myth and converted his family home into La Guarida restaurant.

The restaurant is the most celebrated in the city, and Enrique received the support of Eusebio Leal, the city's historian (Reason #65) when the 1913 timepiece was restored.

Jack Nicholson, Steven Spielberg, Pedro Almodóvar, Beyoncé and Queen Sofía of Spain can all say they have lived the La Guarida experience.

What is the hardest part of being a restaurateur in Havana? The daily challenges—and finding ingredients. I ask myself, what will be the surprise of the day? Once, for example, I had a car full of fresh fish, and that morning, officials decided to tear the road up in front of the restaurant. It can be frustrating. But there are good stories, too. When we first opened, my father used to go buy products for the restaurant by bicycle and transport the stock in a box hitched to the back of his bike. He would bring fresh fish from the local fishermen. To this day, we buy from them, and because of my restaurant, their livelihood has improved. I bought fridges for all of them—I grow, they grow.

What about community projects? I run a summer camp for neighborhood kids (five- to 10-year-olds), where they learn to paint and to cook. On the last day, we always make a big lunch, where the kids do all the cooking and take pride in their creations.

What are your current projects? I have always liked challenges and when I saw the opportunity to restore an old building on El Prado, one of the most emblematic avenues in Havana, I jumped at it. **Ánimas & Virtudes** is an intimate boutique hotel with a small restaurant, and significant wine cave offering a gastronomic experience. [Paseo del Prado 312, btw Ánimas and Virtudes; +535 196 7891]

How do you make the best mojitos? They need to be simple. I am an enemy of adding bitters, because it hides the genuine flavors of the mint, the rum and the lime, which always needs to be freshly squeezed. Balance is everything. Would you like to try one? [I did and it's on my Top Picks list on page 9.]

Favorite restaurant: La Corte del Principe. (Reason #246)

Best sunset: Jardín del Nacional, to reflect and have a drink. (Reason #160)

Best vibe: Rooftop of La Guarida, to relax and have good cocktails and bites.

Favorite festival: The Jazz Fest in December.

Favorite drink: Anything with Havana Club.

A Perfect Combination

125

Havana's grooviest boutique hotel, the brainchild of Sandra Exposito and husband Orlandito Mengual, is a jaw-dropping work of art, with unexpected twists and turns at every step. The mesmerizing **Malecón 663** that opened in 2018 features four rooms, including a suite, each curated by a different local designer and reflecting different styles: retro eclectic, art deco, vintage 1950s and contemporary.

Enter the lobby and behold a hyper-charged kaleidoscope of color and art. Light flowing from the tall double doors highlights vivid hues and intricate details of upcycled vintage furniture and the most creative colonial tile configuration. Its concept store supports young female entrepreneurs, offering a selection of locally crafted design products: captivating jewelry by Brava, custom clothing by Nerea, plush cushions by Titina and Paloma Mengual, who also presents her arresting acrylic

prints and ceramic tiles, and invigorating natural oils by Alba Cosmética.

The journey continues on the second floor for gastronomy and cultural indulgence at café **A lo Cubano**, which offers breakfasts like the *Fuerza arará* (organic yogurt from the farm topped with fresh fruit and detox juices), decadent snacks and meals like the lobster nuggets, confit pork baguette, fish mousseline sandwich on crispy sweet potato and a seafood grill with the catch of the day, all packed with authentic Cuban flavors. Order a coffee or Eminente rum and keep an eye out for a table with Sandra's and my faces on it.

The third floor is entirely occupied by the expansive suite equipped with its own bar, a lounge and huge balcony facing the sea.

The pièce de résistance, its rooftop terrace **No te bañes en el Malecón**, has breathtaking views of Havana's iconic coastline and Centro Habana. Come for sunset when the terrace transforms into a festive four-floored paradise with nightly live music, DJs and themed parties. Creative cocktails include A romper el Coco, a piña colada with Black Tears spiced rum, and the Havana Mule with Havana Club rum, lime juice, ginger beer and macerated chili pepper. Look out for the heir to the throne, Angelo Mengual Abreu, ace operator and maestro of hospitality and style. Insider secret: the terrace is also open for its epic brunch on weekends. [Malecón 663, btw Belascoain and Gervasio; malecon663.com; +535 273 5738]

Sunset Havana Regeneration an architectural tour by bicycle taxi of five of Havana's top terraces—Yarini, Habana 5, La Guarida, Tribe Caribe and Malecón 663—with renowned architect Inclán (page 31), who will unravel the intricacies of his restoration work at each location. There will be cocktails and tapas served, distinctive of each venue. [book tour with Sandra +535 840 5403]

Soviet Fare and Italian Flair on the Waterfront

127 When you drive along the Malecón toward the Morro, look up for the red-and-yellow Soviet flag, and you will spot **Nazdarovie** (A), Havana's only Soviet *paladar*. The idea came from a Canadian lawyer with Slavic roots, who had been living in Cuba for more than 20 years; he wanted to bring back the nostalgia of Russia's communist past for the thousands of Soviet ex-pats who call Cuba home. In 2014, Gregory and Dane, his Cuban wife at the time, opened their gorgeous home—with a prime view onto the Malecón—to the public; they brought in a collective of Russian and Ukrainian chefs to cook up homemade favorites from the Soviet Union. Having lived in Moscow for 10 years, I can say the food is bang-on

Calling All Cigar Aficionados

126 Director of La Casa del Habano Partagas for 19 years, Abel Expósito Díaz opened his home in 2014 to create his own restaurant in one of the most interesting locations in Havana: on a street corner looking down Calle San Lázaro and with a view of the Malecón.

Fully equipped with a smoking salon for the cigar savvy, **Casa Abel** has a great feel with open views, high ceilings, a private dining room, a rooftop terrace and the twirling brass staircase heading up toward the cigar room. The classy bar staff, who don guayaberas, serve up great versions of all the classics—mojitos, piña coladas, Cuba libres as well as excellent espresso. Try the grilled lobster, veggie burgers or the house specialty, *Pollo Casa Abel*—beer-can chicken. [San Lázaro 319, corner San Nicolás; +537 860 6589]

as genuine as you can get. Try one of the best borschts ever served with their homemade *smetana* (sour cream), their hard-to-beat pelmenis and varenikis, juicy chicken Kiev, traditional beef stroganoff or *kolbasa* (sausage), not to mention their deep and soulful homemade Russian black bread. If you are thirsty, they serve up classic cocktails with Stolichnaya and Russian Standard vodka.

You'll be amazed by the colorful Soviet paraphernalia, ranging from propaganda posters to one of the largest matryoshkas

I have ever seen, made in Havana by Cuban artists. On the walls are photographs of Fidel Castro walking in Red Square or sporting a Russian fur hat. Cubans who have studied in the Soviet Union have donated photos that are displayed on the wall on the left when you walk in. Take note of the CCCP hockey jersey on the wall to the left of the bar, a gift from yours truly.

Grab a seat on the balcony and expect to see ambassadors from former Soviet republics. It's a great place, with its merry atmosphere and all! [Malecón 25, btw Paseo del Prado and Cárcel; +537 860 2947]

Feel like Italian instead? To sip on a genuine Aperol Spritz made with prosecco as the sun sets over the Malecón seawall, head to **Marechiaro** (B), which opened in 2022. Enjoy the simple luxury of sitting right on the Malecón and enjoy the genuine Italian fare of Salvatore Ferrone, from Naples, who can whip up seafood paccheri with lobster, clams, octopus and prawns, and pastiera napoletana for dessert. Or maybe a Pizza *salsiccia e friarielli* (sausage and bitter greens) from the wood-burning oven and a glass of their juicy Montepulciano. Unbelievable. [Malecón 217, btw Blanco and Águila]; +535 322 7006]

A Place to be Mindfully Blissful

128

Cuban author Leonardo Padura (Reason #272) says the locals proudly call **El Malecón** the largest park bench in the world. This four-mile (seven-kilometer) long seaside promenade extends from Old Havana to the western tip of Vedado, and if it is not flooded by seaside spill, it is flooded with humanity every single night.

Taking a stroll on the Malecón, or sitting on its concrete edge, is one of life's simplest pleasures. Whether, as Padura says, you are sitting with your back to the sea and watching the ebb and flow of life, or facing the sea and looking inside yourself, this is the number one thing to do in Havana.

If someone is chanting **Maní** and is clutching a bunch of white paper cones, they are selling homemade roasted peanuts. A Herculean trial awaits you in getting the last peanut out of the cone!

Meeting at The Point

129 **La Punta** (A) (The Point) is an irregular plaza on the Malecón at the northern edge of Paseo del Prado, where you find El **Castillo de San Salvador de La Punta** (B). Completed in 1610, it is also known as La Punta, for short. A huge metal chain was attached to the stronghold, linking it to the Castillo de los Tres Reyes del Morro across the bay to protect Havana's harbor from enemy ships. The location of La Punta makes it the perfect place to relax and take in great views of the harbor, the Malecón and Paseo del Prado—even if starry-eyed lovers are impervious to them.

Right across the road to the south of La Punta is **Monumento a los ocho estudiantes de Medicina** (C), a touching memorial to the eight medical students who were falsely accused of profaning a grave; they were executed by a Spanish firing squad at this very spot on November 27, 1871. You can still see the bullet holes in the wall. Every year, on November 27, students march from the steps of the University of Havana (Reason #142) to this sacred spot in their memory.

Taking in Centro Habana

130 Walking—or biking or driving—along **Calle San Lázaro** (A) is one of my all-time favorite things to do in Havana. Just south and parallel to the majestic Malecón, this is its alter ego, the gritty underbelly of Centro Habana. The street stretches across the entire neighborhood connecting Vedado to Old Havana, starting from the University of Havana (Reason #142) all the way to the Paseo del Prado (Reason #116). The equally compelling **Calle Neptuno** (B) also runs right across Centro Habana from east to west beginning at Parque Central all the way up to the university. Take an up-close and personal view into the daily lives of the locals in the most densely populated section of the city to see the raw, the real and the intense.

130A

The Hospital that Made Social Sense

131

Originally slated to be the National Bank of Cuba during the Batista regime, this 23-story building made of light yellow stone was deemed a hospital when construction was completed after the revolution. The **Hermanos Ameijeiras Clinical Surgical Hospital** is named after three brothers who were considered martyrs of the revolution and who lived in the neighborhood. It has an impressive lobby with 50-foot (15-meter) high ceilings and a mural by renowned Cuban-Romanian artist Sandú Darié. This Centro Habana facility is about as centrally located as you can get if you need medical care while in Havana. Open 24/7. [San Lázaro and Belascoaín]

133

A General on Horseback

132 Cuban national hero Antonio Maceo was a revered army general and second-in-command of the Cuban Army of Independence. Known as the Bronze Titan (because of his skin color and his bravery), he fell to Spanish forces in 1896, just two years before Cuba was liberated in 1898. **Parque Antonio Maceo** is located right on the Malecón where it dips south and offers great east-west views of the waterfront. This park is beautiful at sunset, with kids often playing soccer under the towering statue of the valiant statesman on horseback.

Inspiring Architecture

133 My favorite building in Centro Habana, the **Edificio Solimar**, is an eight-story apartment building right off Calle San Lázaro built in 1944 by Manuel Copado. This imaginative modernist structure named after the sun and the sea (*sol y mar*) embodies the waves flowing toward the Malecón wall a few blocks away. Just look up at the undulated balconies to feel the motion of ocean. [Soledad 205, corner Calle San Lázaro]

Hospitals and Medical Clinics for Tourists

Cira García [Calle 20 #4101, corner Avenida 41, Miramar; +537 204 2811 with 24-hour international pharmacy]

Clínica de Siboney [Avenida 17, btw 200 and 202, Siboney; +537 271 1123]

Camilo Cienfuegos [Calle 13 #151, btw L and M, Vedado; +537 835 1212]

CIMEQ [Calle 216 and Avenida 11B, Siboney; +537 273 6548]

Hermanos Ameijeiras Clinical Surgical Hospital (Reason #131)

134A

134A

Raw and Rhythmic Rumba and Steamy Salsa

134 Beginning in 1990, artist Salvador González transformed an entire alley in Centro Habana into a creative masterpiece, building it from scratch with leftover paint and scrap. A colorful artistic hub, **El Callejón de Hamel** (A) is bejeweled with far-out sculptures and street murals, benches made from bathtubs, and small funky shops and restaurants.

Go on Sunday during the day for the Afro-Cuban powwow when the alley comes alive with hypnotic live music capable of summoning the orishas—deities of the Santería religion (Reason #281). For good luck, climb up and sit on the big chair near the western entrance. [Callejón de Hamel, btw Hospital and Aramburu]

Housed in the gorgeous art deco Teatro América, **Casa de La Música Habana** (B) is the melody mecca of Havana with a top of the charts artist roster turning up hot steamy dance nights and a spirited fiesta. [Galiano 255, btw Neptuno and Concordia; +537 860 8297]

A Not-to-Miss Transvestite Show

135 The nightly show is always spectacular, whether it's dancing, singing, comedy or a drag performance at **Cabaret Las Vegas**. Cuban drag queens are especially talented and compelling, the first of whom I photographed in the early 1990s in Havana. The show will blow you away, so get ready for a late night of outlandish fun, which usually gets going around midnight. [Infanta 104, btw Calle 25 and 27]

135

Food to Liberate Your Soul

136

Owner, baker, engineer and Michelin Star Chef Alberto González spent 14 years in Italy working as a chef, as well as studying molecular gastronomy at El Bulli in Spain. He returned to his homeland to open up his own business and on October 10, 2014, on the day Cuban landowner Carlos Manuel de Céspedes liberated the people he enslaved nearly 150 years earlier, Alberto opened up **Salchipizza**, putting an end to the belief that you can't find proper bread in Cuba. Note the photograph of Martin Luther King Jr. upon entering this simple artisanal bakery that specializes in soul food. Alberto creates unique all-natural breads with top-quality ingredients, including various seeds, grains and flours that he brings back in his suitcase from trips to Mexico. At Salchipizza, you can also find amazing celiac-friendly breads, fermented ginger wine, fennel cookies and other concoctions that Alberto whips up on the spot. You can tell so much love is pouring into everything he does! Put this delicious spot on your map. [Calle Infanta 562, btw Valle and Zapata]

Massive Mall and Sleek Boutique

137

Plaza Carlos III (A) is a large multileveled mall that is always crowded and is a scene worth taking in. This is where few tourists roam; local families bring their kids to play in the central playground and hang out at the cafeteria, drink beer, breastfeed, buy electronics, food, cosmetics, clothing or just window-shop.[Avenida Salvador Allende (Avenida Carlos III), btw Árbol Seco and Retiro]

Spiff up your wardrobe with striking vibrant textures and singular design by garb guru Laila Chaaban at her sensational Centro Habana shop **Capicúa** (B). [San Lázaro 55, btw Cárcel and Genios]

Partagás Factory and Cigar Tours

138

Entering into a room of Cuban cigar rollers (*torcedores*) in Havana is like stepping back two centuries as the same techniques are still used today to hand-roll cigars. Rollers sit at small desks piled high with pungent tobacco leaves. There is a lector at the front of the room who reads novels or news excerpts to the workers while they roll and cut; there may also be music pumped throughout the large room.

Keeping track of cigar factories is a bit of a game, as they seem to move around regularly. You absolutely need to buy a ticket for a cigar tour beforehand at any major hotel. Visiting a cigar factory is a must on a trip to Cuba. There are five in Havana, and there are others in the Pinar Del Río Province to the west.

Fábrica de Tabaco **Partagás** (A) [San Carlos 816, corner Peñalver] is where the Partagás rollers relocated to while the Old Havana factory remains closed.

Fábrica de Tabaco **H. Upmann** (B) [Belascoaín 852, btw Desagüe and Peñalver] Having recently served as the Fábrica de Tabaco Romeo y Julieta, this factory is billed as the temporary home of H. Upmann.

Fábrica de Tabaco **La Corona** (C) [20 de Mayo 520, btw Marta Abreu and Línea, Cerro] is the most modern of the cigar factories, and they produce many brands.

Fábrica **El Laguito** (D) [Avenida 146 #2302, btw 21 and 21A, Cubanacán] They roll Cohibas here. This factory is more difficult to access as it is the home of the finest Cuban cigars; it is often off-limits when dignitaries visit.

Casa del Habano Partagas (E) [Bernaza 1, corner O'Reilly; +537 801 1015] is the Habanos store that sells the most cigars in the world. It has existed for 30 years and moved to its new location in 2022, across from the Kempinski Hotel (Reason #86). Open from 9 a.m. to 6 p.m., it has a smoking lounge and bar selling coffee and cocktails, plus lockers for clients who want to store their cigars. Ask for Heri!

A Stroll in South Centro Habana

139 I get a special feeling when I walk on the streets of south **Centro Habana**, just east of Calzada de Infanta and south of Avenida Salvador Allende (Avenida Carlos III). It is a rundown neighborhood, but full of life and—as is the case everywhere in Cuba—the people are friendly and may even invite you to play soccer with them on the street. It's best to stroll late in the afternoon, when the heat starts to abate, and the soft yellow light picks up, leading to magic hour.

Divine Saturday Night Drag Show

140 On Saturday nights, **El Café Cantante**—in the Teatro Nacional—plays host to El Divino, a superb song-and-dance show featuring mind-blowing performances by Havana's star transvestites.

The show is so popular that you will have to wait in line, but don't worry, even that is fun. Cubans are so social that while in line, you will strike up a conversation and be inside before you know it.

Doors open at 11 p.m. and the show starts at around 1 a.m. On other days of the week, it is a live music and dance venue featuring some of the best names in hip-hop, salsa, Afro-Cuban and rock. [Avenida Paseo, corner Calle 39, Plaza de la Revolución]

139

141

140

Revolution Central

141 It's always impressive to drive across the larger-than-life **Plaza de la Revolución** and see the emblematic star-shaped gray-marble José Martí Memorial up close. Not to mention the 60-foot (18-meter) white-marble eponymous statue at its base.

Construction began in 1953, a century after the birth of the national hero. The memorial building includes a museum and observation deck with a panoramic view of the city. One of the largest squares in the world, this is where Fidel Castro hosted political rallies—that drew crowds of more than a million. Depictions of Che Guevara and Camilo Cienfuegos completely covering the facades of government buildings are a reminder that you are in Havana. Stop in the parking lot in the middle of the square to pose with these revolutionaries portrayed by Cuban artist Enrique Ávila.

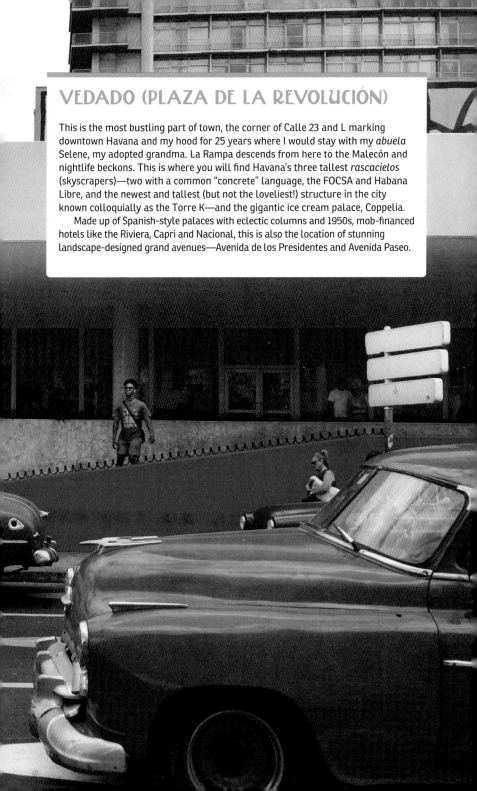

VEDADO (PLAZA DE LA REVOLUCIÓN)

This is the most bustling part of town, the corner of Calle 23 and L marking downtown Havana and my hood for 25 years where I would stay with my *abuela* Selene, my adopted grandma. La Rampa descends from here to the Malecón and nightlife beckons. This is where you will find Havana's three tallest *rascacielos* (skyscrapers)—two with a common "concrete" language, the FOCSA and Habana Libre, and the newest and tallest (but not the loveliest!) structure in the city known colloquially as the Torre K—and the gigantic ice cream palace, Coppelia.

Made up of Spanish-style palaces with eclectic columns and 1950s, mob-financed hotels like the Riviera, Capri and Nacional, this is also the location of stunning landscape-designed grand avenues—Avenida de los Presidentes and Avenida Paseo.

Vedado meaning "do not pass," received its name in the 18th century. When the habaneros lived inside the old city wall, it was not recommended to go to this dangerous area where pirates, filibusters and thieves could be found preparing to attack the city. When the population of Havana increased and spread westward in the 1800s, people began to buy land outside the wall. In 1863 the wall came down.

VEDADO

MALECÓN

187C
187B
187A
CALLE 3
CALLE 5
CALLE 8
CALLE A
CALZADA
200
203
200 174
201
1
1RA
202
CALLE 6
CALLE 4
CALLE 2
LÍNEA
PASEO
CALLE
3RA
178
CALLE 10
CALLE 8
180
CALLE 13

MALECÓN

195 194 191
CALLE 8
CALLE 6
205 181
CALLE A
TÚNEL DE LÍNEA
199
CALLE 10
CALLE 15
CALLE 12
PASAJE
155B
154
196
CALLE 16
CALLE 18
197B
CALLE 21
207
CALLE 13
197A 19
208
CALLE 20
198
CALLE 22
CALLE A
CALLE B
198
AVENIDA 7MA
CALLE 24
204
CALLE 4
CALLE 1
CALLE 17
CALLE E
CALLE 18
CALLE F
CALLE 26
CALLE 12
CALLE 23
CALLE I
CALLE 2
CALLE 3
CALLE 16
CALLE 6
CALLE 28
CALLE 27
CALLE M
CALLE L
CALLE 30
CALLE 29
198
SAN ANTONIO CHIC
CALLE 32

Higher Education on the Hill

142 The oldest university in Cuba, and one of the first in the Americas, La **Universidad de La Habana** (University of Havana) was founded in 1728. It was located in Old Havana until 1902 when it moved to its hilltop home in Vedado, taking over what had been military barracks.

The university educates 20,000 local (and some 400 foreign) students each year. Some of its more famous graduates include Fidel Castro, who studied law here and was heavily engaged in student life; writer Alejo Carpentier (Reason #98); Cuba's first president, Carlos Manuel de Céspedes; and Julio Antonio Mella, founder of the powerful FEU—Unión de la Federación Estudiantil (Federation of University Students).

The main building, known as Aula Magna, was designed by Emilio Heredia. Built in 1911, it features six magnificent frescoes by renowned Cuban painter Armando Menocal. The iconic and domineering bronze *Alma Mater* statue that stands atop the famous 88-step *escalinata* (staircase), which leads up to the university, was created by Czech sculptor Mario Korbel in 1919. Legend has it that the face of the statue bears a striking resemblance to the 16-year-old daughter of the Secretary of Public Works at the time— he happened to be a professor at the university—and the body of the statue is that of a 30-year-old woman.

The university has been a hotbed of students protesting government corruption. Student upheavals triggered the government shutdown of the university twice in the 20th century. President Gerardo Machado closed it in 1933 and many members of the FEU landed in prison. And it was closed again in 1957 by President Fulgencio Batista when violent and bloody confrontations led to deaths of both students and police. That same year, the president of the FEU, José Antonio Echeverría, staged an armed assassination attempt on Batista at the Presidential Palace. Batista survived, but many FEU members did not, including Echeverría, who was shot near the university campus. You can see a

memorial plaque marking the spot where he died on November 27 near Calle L (B), around the corner from the staircase.

One of Fidel Castro's immediate pledges to the Cuban people after the revolution in 1959 was to improve access to education. Shortly thereafter, the University of Havana reopened.

Walk up the steps from San Lázaro and Calle L (or run up and down them, like I do!) without missing the retro lamps at the bottom, and take a tour of the campus by going past the majestic neoclassical columns.

Foreigners can take a plethora of classes at the university. I once took a valuable intensive course to top up my Spanish. Courses that can last from three weeks up to nine months are available, including law, Cuban history, salsa or casino-style dance classes and more. See the university webpage (uh.cu) for details. [San Lázaro and Calle L]

Don Quixote Au Naturel

143

Parque Don Quijote is a cute little space in the middle of Calle 23 with an impressive impressionist statue of a nude Don Quixote, the backdrop of nonstop selfies. This unique work of art, made by Sergio Martínez Sopeña in 1980, was very avant-garde at the time because the technique used to create this rough expression—welding thick iron bars together—was a first in Cuba.

Sit under the large leafy trees to take advantage of the shade and be sure to note the beautiful scale of the sculpture to the square; they fit together so neatly. [Calle 23 and Calle J]

A Green Leafy Pause at the Villa of General Gómez

145 **Quinta de los Molinos** is a magnificent 12-acre enchanted garden that is the perfect refuge from the urban buzz of Havana. Musicians come here to practice their wind instruments in the shade, under the trees. It is also the city's oldest botanical garden with more than 150 species of plants, birds, reptiles and some other wildlife unique to Cuba.

Central to the property is the *quinta* (villa) itself, which was the residence of Cuban War of Independence commander General Máximo Gómez. The garden gets its name from the tobacco mill (*molino*) that once stood on the site.

Quinta de los Molinos underwent a 10-year renovation before reopening in 2014. Take a walk on the pathways with lush vegetation at your sides and enjoy a break from ubiquitous exhaust fumes on the city streets. And don't miss the butterfly house where rare species flutter freely. [Avenida Carlos III, btw Avenida de la Independencia and Infanta]

Bonaparte Art

144 Even if you are not at all interested in Napoleon, you must see the **Museo Napoleónico** purely for its architectural value. Its dreamy courtyard and balconies give a rare and prized view of Vedado and Centro Habana. It was built by illustrious Cuban architects Evelio Govantes and Félix Cabarrocas, renowned for Capitolio Nacional (Reason #111), Casa de la Amistad (Reason #189), and Xanadu Mansion (Reason #300).

Once staffed with more than a dozen workers, the magnificent four-story Florentine renaissance mansion belonged to Dr. Orestes Ferrara Marino—a deputy of early 20th-century President Gerardo Machado, who lived there alone with his wife.

In 1961 the house was converted into the Napoleon Museum and it now houses the most complete collection of Napoleonic art found outside of France.

The collection belonged to Julio Lobo Olavarría, a huge sugar magnate and Napoleon fanatic, who acquired his vast collection from Europe and the United States. Check out the monocular used by Napoleon in Saint Helena to spy on British ships, the revolver he used to fight Russians in the Battle of Borodino, his famous bicorne hat and otherworldly period pieces decorating each room. [San Miguel 1159, corner Ronda]

Food Ambassador

147 Your culinary adventure in Havana starts right here, starring philosophical and passionate chef-owner **Raulito Bazuk**, who converted his family home into a restaurant in 2017 and named it **Grados** after the Hermann Hesse poem "Stages," which he says perfectly summed up his life with its poignant metaphors. Raulito learned to cook by watching his mom and grandma create masterpieces with whatever was at hand due to shortages. "Cooking in Cuba is in some ways an act of resistance and survival. We are obliged to be imaginative, and are always up to the challenge."

Startling creative concoctions include the Bazuka Magical Drink, homemade gingerbug soda, mango and pineapple infusion and *aguardiente* (or as a mocktail); and the True Amigos: coconut liqueur, Santiago rum, lime, molasses and sparkling water. Prepare yourself for their innovative approach to fish—Pescado & Petróleo (Fish & Petroleum)—homemade smoked fish with a pitch-black sauce made of black beans, fish stock and herbs; and the house favorite Lamb & Prú casserole with tamale.

"To find new light that old ties cannot give," wrote Hesse. "In all beginnings dwells a magic force for guarding us and helping us to live." [Calle E 562, btw 23 and 25; +535 463 0656]

Unifying Drink

146 **El Bodegón de Theodoro** is a tavern—just one block away from the University of Havana—where Fidel Castro and other students met to conspire against Fulgencio Batista's dictatorship. While pretending to do homework, they were secretly plotting attacks. Legend has it that the owner, Theodoro, helped the revolutionary cause by stashing guns and armbands of the *26 de Julio* (26th of July) movement inside empty beer barrels. The tavern also served as a place to hide for Castro and other student leaders when police were in pursuit. You can still see the beer barrels in question, while getting a lingering sense of the 1940s and '50s.

After the revolution, one of the bartenders at the tavern invented the Negrón, a drink that was meant to quell racism, by symbolically bringing blacks and whites together. The amity mixture consisted of cola (the black), lime juice (the white), rum, sugar, *hierbabuena* and ice—humanity happily united in a glass!

Grunge alert: Bring your own toilet paper and hand wipes. [San Lázaro, corner Calle N]

Mabel Ma Belle

148 Born in Cienfuegos in 1986, **Mabel Poblet** is one of the most exciting contemporary visual artists of our time. The dramatically emotional effect of her art, which is rooted in her own life journey, surprises those who know her shy nature. She skillfully intertwines translucent materials—such as glass, vials, plexiglass, mirrors and acetate—to reflect her intricate purpose to the viewer. Mabel's art is a perspective interplay between transience and infinity. It focuses on themes such as individual memory, experience and fragility of life as well as social and political dimensions connected to her identity as a Cuban artist.

Mabel graduated from the Instituto Superior de Arte in 2012 and from the Academia Nacional de Bellas Artes San Alejandro with highest honors. In 2017 she was among the artists representing Cuba at the Venice Biennale.

Walking into her spacious Vedado studio is a multisensory, quasi-cinematic experience: lights, camera, action! Works made of hundreds of cutouts from photographs, bent precisely then assembled in a grid pattern, form an immersive, mesmerizing mosaic that—impossibly—forms her own lips, or her portrait. Or a mandala. Or underwater.

It is impossible not to be drawn into the complex layers of her masterpieces. In awe, I said to her, "Mabel you are incredible." She answered in her bashful way, "I don't think so." Which makes you want to love her even more!

I always leave her studio feeling renewed, refreshed, excited and inspired.

[To visit Mabel's studio email studio@mabelpobletstudios.com; WhatsApp +535 293 2262]

The Heart of Vedado

149

When it was built in 1958, this was the tallest and largest hotel in Latin America, the "it" spot to be in Havana, overflowing with visiting celebrities. Standing tall over Vedado on Calle L and 23, the busiest corner of the city, **Tryp Habana Libre Hotel** run by Meliã has never gone out of style. Originally the Havana Hilton, operated by Americans and opened by Conrad Hilton himself, this 27-story modern architectural centerpiece became Fidel Castro's headquarters in 1959. It was here, in suite 2324 ("La Castellana"), that he led the revolution, and if you look up from the outside at the top left of the building, you will see the three rooms that made up his command center: they are the only three windows where glass was not added, to keep it original to its time. You can take an exclusive tour of the Castellana suite where everything remains intact.

The grand public spaces, including the modern lobby and mezzanine, still capture the hotel's imposing and iconic stature, as does the landmark blue-and-white mural by eminent modernist artist Amelia Peláez on the facade. You can wander inside to see more masterful murals by Alfredo Sosabravo and René Portocarrero.

If you want to (literally) dance under the stars to live music, the place to go is **El Turquino** on the 25th floor. When you walk into this rather posh nightclub, smack in front of you is a grandiose circular bar flanked by 1950s barstools. But most spectacular are the views of Havana on either side and the retractable roof that opens to the sky and the cosmos at midnight. It's breathtaking every time.

Silver Screen Sensation

150

The impressive **Cine Yara**, a landmark since it was built in 1947, was originally the Teatro Warner Radiocentro operated by Warner Bros. Cubans love to go to the movies and to this day the Yara is still the city's primary picture palace for homegrown and foreign films. It is also the key venue for the annual Havana Film Festival in December and it hosts many live music shows. The Yara is a hot spot, and it deserves to occupy this prime street corner.

From the sidewalk, you can't miss its iconic red modernist facade with its retro "YARA" lettering. And for practically nothing you can watch a film inside the resplendent red 1,650-seat theater and feel, well... privileged. Films are projected on a humongous screen—at one time it was an official Cinerama (three 35-millimeter projections displayed on a curved screen), and Spanish-language movies have English subtitles, which helps because the Cuban dialect is unbelievably quick.

Be sure to pick up some popcorn from a street vendor on La Rampa before you head in! [Calle L 363, corner Calle 23]

An Ice Cream Palace for the People

151 I was taken with **Coppelia** the moment I first set foot in Havana in 1989, and it has become very nostalgic for me. I love its iconic nature, the modernist architecture, the lush garden of palm and banyan trees and watching the ice cream feast unfold as platters piled high of unimaginable quantities of multicolored scoops are devoured at each table. With Havana's heat, this just might be the best ice cream moment you'll ever have.

For the modest price, there are a lot of patient takers. The customary queue could mean up to a two-hour wait in the blaring sun, but socializing while waiting for this national treat is a part of the experience. In its heyday, Coppelia served up more than 25 flavors; nowadays, though you may be lucky and find caramel or orange pineapple, the main choices are vanilla, strawberry and chocolate, the last two forming the name of Cuba's most famous and edgy film, *Fresa y Chocolate*, which has a memorable scene inside the parlor.

Built in 1966 with a capacity of 1,000, and taking up two entire city blocks, this ice cream parlor is one of the largest in the world. It is shaped like a flying saucer and made up of five huge white granite disks,

each partitioned with magnificent wood and tinted glass panels attached to a spiral staircase. It is all elevated on cement pillars and there is an open space on the ground floor with three long curved ice cream bars and 1950s-style stools. You have to see it to believe it. Simply incredible!

Coppelia was a personal project of Fidel Castro's because he loved ice cream. Angered by the U.S. blockade in the early 1960s, he decided to create the biggest and best ice cream parlor in the world. He hired renowned Cuban architect Mario Girona and brought in top-of-the-line machines from the Netherlands and Sweden. He asked the Canadian ambassador at the time to ship him dozens of containers of ice cream from Howard Johnson's to try different flavors.

Celia Sánchez, Fidel Castro's comrade-in-arms, gave Coppelia its name, after her favorite ballet. [Calle 23 and L]

Just beside Coppelia on Calle 23 is an open-air market offering traditional handicrafts.

The Heart of the City

152 **La Rampa** (A), the legendary main drag in Vedado, is the section of Calle 23 that descends like a ramp to the sea stretching from Calle L to the Malecón. A lot of vibrant activity is crammed into these five blocks and it has long been a central meeting point in the city.

Calle L and 23, the top of La Rampa, is the fabulous epicenter of Vedado, where each corner is abuzz: Cine Yara, the Habana Libre, Coppelia and the Artex souvenir shop.

The sidewalk here is embedded with precast granite and bronze contoured art displays, including works by Wifredo Lam, Amelia Peláez and Luis Martínez Pedro that date back to the 1960s. In the middle of the stretch you will find **Pabellón Cuba** (B), a large semi-open exhibit space with huge concrete slabs and columns built right into the hillside, home to cultural activities and festivities.

Farther down La Rampa is the landmark red British telephone booth marking the entrance to Havana's famous jazz club **La Zorra y El Cuervo** (C) (The Fox and the Crow), an intimate, dark and atmospheric basement venue, where top jazz musicians perform every night except Monday: the show starts at 11:30 p.m. Truly an impressive, must-see jazz scene. [Calle 23, btw N and O; +537 833 2402]

From the red telephone booth, turn onto Calle O and walk one block to **Neder Café** (D) for an ice latte, a milkshake, frappé lemonade, fast food and to catch a sports game on the big screen TV. [Calle O #252, btw 25 and 27]

¿Quién es el último? Who's the last in line? Cubans are pros at the lineup. No need to wait in single file! Just ask ¿Quién es el último? When you find them, you become el último and you can wait leisurely keeping an eye on the person before you. Next person who shows up asking ¿Quién es el último?, you respond Soy yo (It's me).

The Existential Artist

153

Talented and trendy contemporary painter **Gustavo Echevarría**, aka **Cuty Ragazzone**, is exhibited all over Havana, from the hippest restaurants to the most luxurious homes. He is famous for his renditions of women squatting on the toilet that form part of his series called *Baño Ajeno* (someone else's bathroom). "But why?" I asked him. "It's something in my subconscious," he explained.

Cuty and I spoke in the seaside town of Gibara about his love for Havana and the *habaneros*:

"What I love about the people is the way they handle themselves and the way they think. I like that they know *how* to wait. They may not know what they are waiting for, but it doesn't matter, they are always waiting and hoping for something good. The weather helps a lot... The sea and the sun are not unique; it exists in many places, but the heat and the sun here produce a distinctive sweat. It emits a shine, like an aura or an illusion that makes people look like tireless workers—and they are beautiful.

"Everybody thinks their country is the best in the world, as I do. Cuba has a distinctive magic that gives us a special feeling. We don't know if we are in the past or the future.

"Do you know what is good about this country? We know how to live in the present. We say that today and tomorrow is *now*. This way of thinking penetrates you like a bacteria, like a virus, and it turns into love, a love for living in the present.

"Habaneros are noble. You might think that with all the problems and hardships they have had, they might be antagonistic. But they stay noble. Suffering and sacrifice have not remodeled their personality, it has kept them sincere and kind. It's what I like about the people and it's important that they don't lose their civility and graciousness—and they haven't!"

Cuty's favorite restaurants: Yarini (Reason #56) O'Reilly 304, El del Frente (Reason #105), Al Carbón (Reason #89), El Antonia (Reason #109), Neder Café (Reason #152).

Visit Cuty's studio where you can peruse and procure some of his unique art. Call ahead for an appointment. [Calle 25 #216, apartment 10, btw N and O; +535 236 6169]

"We were told after the revolution that we are all equal, but we realized that we are not. We have all kinds of differences. But in the end, deep down, we all feel equal."
Cuty Ragazzone

The Heart of the Gay Community

154

Everything changed for the LGBTQ+ community in Cuba when Raúl Castro's daughter **Mariela Castro Espín** became an advocate, championing LGBTQ+ rights. Because of her influence and strong stand, the gay community lives more freely, and has an improved relationship with the police. Mariela created the National Center for Sex Education **CENESEX** [Calle 10 #460, btw 19 and 21], an LGBTQ+ resource center that campaigns for effective AIDS prevention, and recognition and acceptance of LGBTQ+ human rights. In 2005, Mariela proposed that Cubans be able to have sex-reassignment surgery and have their gender recognized. The measure, which became law in 2008, allows for sex-change surgery without charge. In 2022, same-sex marriages, same-sex adoptions and nonprofit surrogacy became legal here: of course Mariela Castro was a staunch advocate of the measure. Approved in a novel landmark referendum, the law replaces the 1975 Código de la Familia (Family Code). Cuba is now the 34th country in the world in which same-sex marriage is legal.

The International Day Against Homophobia and Transphobia is celebrated annually with a vivid parade that takes place in the city area around May 17.

Two-Wheel Transport

155

There are no bike paths and little bike culture in Havana, as drivers are king of the roads—so be careful while riding and crossing the streets in general. Also be aware that cars will inevitably spew black smoke in your face—and keep an eye out for the especially huge potholes or uncovered maintenance holes, which make safety optional! Biking is one of my favorite things to do in Havana and it's the best way to see this raw and real urban landscape up close and personal.

Stop in at **Vélo Cuba** (A) [Prado 20, btw San Lázaro and Capdevilla, Old Havana; +535 282 5148; veloencuba.com] and the almost exclusively female team of professional bicycle mechanics, headed by founder and president Nayvis Díaz Labaut, will get you outfitted with sturdy bikes with shock absorbers capable of withstanding Havana's roads. Countrywide tours are also on offer.

For guided bike tours in English, French or Spanish, rentals or repairs, head to the first bicycle rental company in Cuba, **RutaBikes** (B) [Calle 16 #152, btw 13 and 15, Vedado; +535 247 6633; rutabikes.com] founded by Ebert Trujillo in 2012.

Citykleta is a nonprofit created by Yasser González that promotes cycle culture and sustainability in Havana through events, festivals and free workshops that teach women how to ride and repair bikes. Donations of bicycle parts and accessories are welcome. [info@citykleta.org; +535 565 2579; citykleta.org]

Chivo (C) means "goat" in Spanish but it is also Cuban slang for bicycle, and the name of a passion project by Alfonso Fernández Castillo, who specializes in antique bike rentals, tours and repairs and is a connoisseur of the little-known history of bicycles in Cuba. Look out for a museum of sustainable transport and peace of mind to come. In the meantime, Chivo has set up bike rental spots sprinkled around Old Havana. [Main Office: Oficios 212, btw Muralla and Teniente Rey; +535 325 4282]

155 C

Penthouse Cuisine

157

One of the prettiest restaurants in all of Havana is the charming **Café Laurent**, with its inviting terrace perched up on the top floor of a four-story apartment building.

Riding up a vintage elevator—it is usually working—the doors open onto a pristine setting of white tablecloths, incandescent white drapes billowing in the breeze, and yellowed wallpaper of 1950s newspaper ads. Soft crosscurrents that drift through the dining room bring with them a magical and soothing feel. Plus breathtaking views of the Straits of Florida, where an occasional cruise ship or freighter may be in sight, makes this *paladar* dreamingly intoxicating. But we are not here to find nirvana, we are here to eat. And drink!

Here are some flavorsome suggestions: for starters the octopus or beef carpaccio, then the garlic-infused, slow-cooked lamb served with a creamy mint reduction, or the red snapper topped with clams and shrimp in a green salsa and, for dessert, their tangy lemon tart! [Calle M 257, btw 19 and 21, Penthouse; +537 831 2090]

The Hidden Bar

156

La Roca, with its famed bright stained glass facade and concrete canopied drive-thru entrance, was a 1950s mobster haunt. Nowadays the restaurant, with its formal dining room and regular comedy nights, is a little past its prime, but feels timeless when you cross the threshold, turn left and enter the pitch-black bar. Cubans playing hooky from work at the nearby radio station sit in the corner unnoticed drinking Santiago de Cuba 11-year-old rum, surrounded by Real Madrid and Barça soccer flags. Drop in after lunch at Café Laurent (Reason #157) and feel a little naughty, like the rest of its patrons in this dark clandestine tavern. [Calle 21, corner M]

Breakfast at the Capri

158 Traditionally it hasn't been easy to find breakfast spots in Havana, but the early morning food fog in the city is lifting and local restaurateurs have woken up to the fact that visitors really do enjoy their morning meal out!

The **Hotel Capri**, stunningly restored after a massive 10-year renovation project, is known for its iconic rooftop pool and bar (think the movie *I Am Cuba* by Mikhail Kalatozov) and their legendary nightclub Salon Rojo del Capri. The hotel also boasts a bountiful breakfast buffet. To get there, take the scenic route through the marvelous 1950s-style lobby, or enter by the side entrance on Calle N, and you will behold a luncheonette of a bygone era: retro pastel colors ubiquitous in Havana, vintage tables and vinyl chairs, and wait staff in nifty uniforms.

The buffet is constantly replenished with fresh pastries, smoked salmon, cold cuts, hot oatmeal, and plenty of fresh fruit. Also on offer are celestial espresso, *café con leche* (latte), an endless supply of fresh-brewed coffee, and a vast choice of fresh fruit juices and smoothies—guava, pineapple, orange, and *fruta bomba*. [Calle 21, btw Calle N and O]

Riding in a Coconut-Shaped Rickshaw

159 There is nothing like a **coco taxi ride** along the Malecón, Havana's seaside boulevard (Reason #128). With the sea on one side and fabulous colonial architecture on the other, a ride in these yellow-shelled windowless cabs gives you an up close and personal view of the city.

Buzzing around on three wheels with a helmeted driver, a coco taxi feels more like an amusement park ride than a regular cab. The fleet is state-owned, so the vehicles are standardized and you can usually be guaranteed a good chat as well. That is if you can hear above the roaring engine at full throttle! The black bulbous diesel exhaust fumes you will inhale are also a downside, but by no means a reason to avoid this exhilarating jaunt.

They used to be cheaper than regular cabs, but not anymore, so best to negotiate the fare before heading out on this "coconutty" ride. [Found across town and notably at the Meliã Cohiba, Habana Libre, Hotel Nacional and Hotel Inglaterra.]

160A

Glamour Lives On

160 On a warm Havana evening, there are few spots that compare with the breezy garden terrace at the **Hotel Nacional** (A), with music playing, peacocks roaming and the incredible seafront view. Perched on a rocky cliff overlooking the Straits of Florida, the imposing hotel—built in 1930—with its unusual mélange of art deco and neoclassical styles, has hosted politicians, celebrities and high rollers, including Winston Churchill, Rita Hayworth and Charles "Lucky" Luciano. Go to the Hall of Fame at the **Vista al Golfo Bar** to see photos of Johnny Weissmuller, Buster Keaton, Tom Mix, John Wayne, Fred Astaire, Tyrone Power, Nat King Cole and Josephine Baker.

Spend an extravagant evening and step back into the 1950s at the **Cabaret Parisien** (B), where you can dine, watch its sizzling show, and learn how to dance afterward or retire for a nightcap at the tiny **Winston Churchill Bar**, tucked away on the ground floor beside the main dining room. There is no place like the Nacional. [Calle 21 and O]

Authentic Cuban Bolero Jazz Club

161 This bar, whose name means "the one-eyed cat," is a classic late-night jazz spot reminiscent of a 1920s New York club. **El Gato Tuerto** has been Havana's prime bohemian retreat for more than half a century. The best of the best—including the legendary Omara Portuondo of the Buena Vista Social Club—have performed here. Friday and Saturday nights are most popular at this intimate *bolero* and *nueva trova* venue. [Calle O, btw 17 and 19]

161

Vintage Car Club

162 In the land of the moving museum, there are car buffs who keep their vehicle so true to its roots, they will scour the Earth to find original parts for their pre-revolutionary pride and joy. Welcome to the **Club de Autos Antiguos y Clásicos—A lo Cubano**, a group that meets every Saturday at the Hotel Comodoro (Reason #253) as of 3 p.m. and the second Sunday of every month at the Tropicana (Reason #219) at 11 a.m. to fraternize with other aficionados, get intel on car parts, and show off their automobiles. [You can contact car club president Alberto Gutiérrez for updates. +535 245 9250]

Dance with the *Habaneros*

163 Welcome to **Skyline** (A) [Calzada #101, btw L and M]. This happening rooftop bar overlooking the U.S. Embassy (Reason #164) is a great place to mix with the community and catch some standout musical acts. Step outside on the terrace and see the prime view of the Malecón and the sea beyond.

Bar ILUXION (B) [Calle 17, btw E and F] is a 1990s throwback with its pseudo-contemporary style, but it looks otherworldly when juxtaposed with its turn-of-the-century Vedado neighbors. Set in a completely renovated neoclassical home with a slick white minimalist interior and a white facade upon which different colors are flashed at night, this busy nightclub includes a VIP area and bottle service on the 2nd floor. Cram in and dance with locals to A-list acts in this one-of-a-kind nightclub.

Almost Buddies

164

Built in 1953 under U.S. President Dwight D. Eisenhower, the **U.S. Embassy** (A) [Calzada 55, btw L and M] was padlocked after the 1959 Cuban revolution and remained so until 1977. It was then known as the U.S. Interests Section, operating under the auspices of the Swiss Embassy until 2015 when Barack Obama and Raúl Castro "made up," and the embassy reopened.

While the two countries were quarreling, the Interests Section ran anti-Cuba propaganda on a huge ticker on the facade of their modernist six-story concrete-and-glass landmark building, which commandeers a prime location on the Malecón. In response, Fidel Castro erected 140 flagpoles with black flags to hide the vitriolic American newsflashes.

Protestódromo (B) was a stage for protests over American actions in regards to Cuba. In recent years, the space has been used for pop concerts and events with international DJs.

After the revolution, the Cuban public was so angry at the former American mob-influenced Batista government that it destroyed everything in sight that was considered a symbol of imperialism, including casinos at the Capri, Sevilla and Plaza hotels and parking meters throughout the city. The crowd even pulled down the eagle crowning the Monument to the Victims of the U.S.S. *Maine* that is missing to this day.

The **Monument to the Victims of the U.S.S. *Maine*** (C), built by architects Govantes and Cabarrocas, honors the 266 victims of a warship that exploded in Havana harbor in 1898. The incident served as the pretext for the United States to declare war on Spain, starting the Spanish-American War.

A statue of a defiant **José Martí and child** (D) (baby Elián) placed by the waterfront depicts the national hero pointing his finger vehemently toward the American Embassy, shielding the innocent child from "imperialistic forces of evil and decay"—as if to say that history should not be forgotten.

This tragicomedy nearly ended when Barack Obama visited in 2016 "to bury the last remnant of the Cold War in the Americas." Then came Donald Trump, who hardened the U.S. stance again, a position with which President Joe Biden seems comfortable, but there is a lingering optimism that things will find a balance.

The Mini City

166

Built in 1956, the **FOCSA** was a huge architectural feat for Cuban engineers; it was one of the largest reinforced concrete structures in the world. FOCSA was a novelty in its time, conceived "à la Le Corbusier" as a self-contained island within a city with everything at arm's length for its inhabitants: stores, restaurants, a bank, a pharmacy, businesses and a 500-car indoor parking garage. This 39-story residential structure was, at 397 feet (121 meters), the tallest building in Cuba, until 2023 when Torre K superseded it with 42 floors reaching 505 feet (154 meters).

You can see one of the best 360-degree views of the city from **La Torre**, FOCSA's rooftop restaurant-bar. It is really quite surreal. The best time to go for dinner or drinks is at sunset.

There is also a restaurant on the main floor called **El Emperador**. It is as regal as can be, and has maintained its original ambiance even after a huge presidential makeover. As the story goes, back in the 1970s, when Cuba hosted a Latin American summit, Chilean President Salvador Allende called up Fidel Castro personally to tell him how excited he was to come back to Havana and go to his favorite restaurant, Emperador. Following the exchange, Castro asked his men if they could reserve a table for President Allende when he came to town. The bad news was that the restaurant had been derelict for a number of years. Castro ordered a complete refurbishment that was finished just in time for Allende's visit—and it has been open ever since.

Check out Emperador's amazingly long and striking cocktail bar and equally long affordable cocktail list. The lavish old-world restaurant specializes in old-fashioned international cuisine served formally, including a number of dishes and desserts flambéed at your table. [Calle 17, btw M and N; +537 832 4998]

Enter the Groove

165

Welcome to **Tempo**, Vedado's new hot spot, set in a mansion curated to transport you to the glamorous 1920s: antique refurbished furniture, sparkling chandeliers and a ritzy bar in illuminated gold. Featuring cozy nooks and an Astroturf chill zone in the front yard, the real pièce de resistance is a playful wall mural in the bar symbolizing equality, inclusivity and Havana's cultural diversity.

Standout beverages include "120 bpm," with tequila, ginger and lemon, and "Presto Spritz," with a syrup made from dehydrated rose petals. The menu is stacked with shareable treats, such as coconut milk ceviche and peanut-seared chicken fingers. [Calle B 153, btw Linea and Calzada]

You Got to LOVE It

167 Young Cuban musicians Ana María Torres Abella and María Carla Puga Marín started making jewelry during the pandemic out of beads and string they found in their homes. They say that no brand made the trendy colorful beaded pieces they envisioned wearing. Their designs caught on: friends began asking for their pearl, quartz and crystal creations. Eventually they began designing crocheted purses, tops and skirts as well. The outlet for their talent is **AMA**, a boutique café they opened in 2020, fusing art, fashion and healthy living with locally sourced organic foods and smoothie bar. Try the Tokyo Pasta, a noodle dish with seafood and arugula, along with a detox juice blending beet, pineapple, cucumber, celery, carrot and ginger and feel the love and joy the brand and the space aim to embody. [Calle 19 #106, btw L and M; +535 404 0724]

Ink-Credible Experience

168 Founded in 2013 by Ana Lyem, one of the first female tattoo artists in Cuba, and Alberto Ferrer, **Zenit Tattoo Studio** is not just any tattoo parlor. According to my son Luka (AKA @rondobanks), it is one of the most unique spaces in Havana; they're always cooking up new projects— painting murals, performance art, exhibitions, and of course tattoos and piercings. Tattoo artist extraordinaire Mr. Black, the Legend, has not only left his artistic imprint on many members of our family but has also become like family to us. [Calle D, #205 (altos/penthouse), btw Línea and 11; +535 411 5486]

E-bike Flyby

169

The funnest and most exhilarating way to see Havana is with **Cubyke**, the electric bike company owned by bon vivant Martin Staub who brought his joie de vivre and German prowess to the island. Cubyke hit the streets in 2017 after Martin, who learned welding in a previous life as a miner, and a friend built all the steel bikes by hand, setting them apart from other hybrids by incorporating German motors, German batteries, a patented secure frame and irrefutably cool style.

As music booms from a portable speaker, the electrifying tours immerse you in local surroundings so you can experience the dynamic city firsthand, with stops for snack and drinks at the latest hangouts. "It's all about the feeling and vibe," says Martin. "I'm always scouting new places. I love to discover Havana every day. It's my passion."

Pick from a plethora of tours, such as: Deep in La Habana (insider secrets!), Mafia Tour, Revolution Tour, Hang Like Hemingway, La Habana Campo (Santa Fe, beach at Barbacoa), La Habana Gourmet & Cocktail Tour and La Habana by Night. [Calle 21 #507A, btw D and E; +535 012 9620; www.cubyke.com]

Jewish Life in Havana

170

It's interesting to know that Cuba was one of the few places in the world that welcomed Jews escaping Nazi-occupied Europe. Once 20,000 strong, the Jewish community today numbers about 1,200 across the island, with most living in Havana, which is home to the largest and most active synagogue. Led by beloved Adela Dworin, **Sinagoga Beth Shalom** (A) [Calle I, corner 13] is part of a complex referred to as the *Patronato*. It comprises a library, clinic, community center and Sunday school. You'll recognize it immediately by its fantastic 1950s modernist architecture, with a Star of David on the facade and elegant front doors covered in Semitic symbols.

Just a few blocks away, the **Centro Hebreo Sefaradi** (B) (Sephardic Hebrew Center) [Calle 17, corner E] houses a small museum; it recounts the history of the Cuban Jewish community, and an exhibit called "We Remember" is dedicated to victims of the Holocaust.

Both synagogues welcome tourists to take part in all celebrations; they also organize guided tours.

Intimate yet Intense Live Music Venue

171

All the great Cuban contemporary musicians play at **Café Teatro Bertolt Brecht**, including Cimafunk, Havana D'Primera, Toques del Río, Telmary (in photo above), Raúl Paz and Alain Pérez (Reason #262), among others. Formerly the Jewish Community Center, inside the main synagogue in the city, this basement venue is now secular with live music shows and theatrical performances throughout the week. There is a cool bar at the back as well as a small outdoor café on the 2nd-floor terrace, where you're sure to see famous local actors and artists gathering for java in the afternoon before rehearsal. [Calle 13, btw I and J]

172A

Artful Galleries

172

Galería Habana (A) [Línea 460, btw E and F], Havana's oldest and most prestigious gallery, was founded in 1962 to promote Cuba's avant-garde artists and it remains at the forefront of the contemporary art scene in the city.

Welcome to **El Apartamento** (B) [Calle 15 #313, apt 3, corner H], a contemporary art hub located on the 3rd floor of a Vedado apartment building. It is a sleek workshop-gallery that represents over 20 hot artists, including Flavio Garciandía, Diana Fonseca, Ariamna Contino, Roberto Diago, Rocío García, and Reynier Leyva Novo. They also promote young up-and-coming artists who've recently graduated from ISA (Instituto Superior de Arte). Each corner of this modern space surprises you with a different medium, whether it's installations, photography or paintings. If you are looking to buy something unique and unusual, this is the place to go.

172B

National Union of Writers and Artists of Cuba

173

If you are interested in following the tracks of the post-revolutionary intelligentsia, you must visit **UNEAC** (Unión de Escritores y Artistas de Cuba), created in 1962 to unite artists and great thinkers with the aim of preserving Cuban culture. In the glory days it was not uncommon to encounter such figures as writers José Lezama Lima and Alejo Carpentier, painter René Portocarrero, ceramist Alfredo Sosabravo, ballerina Alicia Alonso, and President Fidel Castro here. They attended conferences, poetry readings, painting exhibits and music concerts in the creative ambiance of this cultural center. Visiting guests included Turkish poet Nâzim Hikmet and Chilean poet Pablo Neruda.

Go past the gates toward the mansion and take a walk through the lush garden to see the statue of poet, and the first president of UNEAC, Nicolás Guillén. Then grab a coffee or beer (not many offerings!) on their outdoor terrace **Hurón Azul** and mix with an eclectic crowd of literati and tourists. Try to catch live music—be it nueva trova, rumba, bolero or son—and dance right there on the patio under the leafy trees with the veranda of the mansion serving as the stage. [Calle 17 #351, corner H]

For Veggie Lovers

174 Havana's pioneer vegetarian eatery has been going strong since 2013 and is THE place for healthy, innovative veggie and vegan fare. As you enter the harmonious simplicity of **Camino al Sol**, homemade dishes inside a refrigerated countertop display case are ready to enjoy: yucca gnocci with stewed vegetables, beetroot and sweet potato tart, chickpea cheese, a sweet potato-and-coconut dessert called *boniatillo* and fresh juices: mango-ginger, tamarind, guava, pineapple and hibiscus. Take some of the magic home; there is multicolored in-house pasta for sale at the front counter—beet, spinach, moringa, turmeric, spirulina, you name it. [Calle 3ra #363, btw Paseo and Calle 2; +537 832 1861]

174

175

History on the Avenue

175 Calle G, officially known as **Avenida de los Presidentes**, is a beautiful boulevard lined with meticulously trimmed trees and shrubs that surround a string of statues of historic Latin American political figures. Among the honored are Salvador Allende, Benito Juárez, Omar Torrijos and Simón Bolívar. Crowning the top of the boulevard is José Miguel Gómez, Cuba's second president.

When getting around Vedado, it helps to know that all streets east of Paseo have letter names (Calle A, Calle B, etc.), while to the west even numbers are used (Calle 2, Calle 4, etc.) all the way to the end of the neighborhood, by the river. All cross streets are odd-numbered: the higher the number, the farther you are from the coast.

Culture Club

176 Founded in 1961 by Haydée Santamaría—a Moncada* attack survivor—**La Casa de las Américas** is a brilliant institution that promotes Latin American art and literature. This architectural hybrid of art deco details in a church-like layout is the perfect place for concerts, conferences, exhibits, dance, theater, music, poetry... Just about anything cultural can be found here. Famous visiting icons of the past included Gabriel García Márquez, Pablo Neruda, Mario Vargas Llosa, Victor Jara, Juan Manuel Serrat and Roque Dalton.

La Casa de las Americas is also the birthplace of *la nueva trova*, the musical movement created by singers Silvio Rodríguez and Pablo Milanés, and sponsored by Haydée Santamaría.

Check casadelasamericas.org for scheduling. [Calle 3 #52, corner G]

* Moncada: Military barracks in Santiago de Cuba that were attacked in 1953 by Fidel Castro to kickstart the revolution.

Beautiful Concrete

177 **Edificio Girón**, known locally as *F y Malecón* (the corner where it is located), may be an eyesore to some, but I absolutely adore this Soviet brutalist structure. Built in the 1960s as an apartment building, its base reminds me of Le Corbusier's Cité Radieuse in Marseille. Girón, named after the bus company that housed its employees here, was the surname of a 16th-century French pirate. One of the first buildings that was commissioned after the revolution by the new government, this modern-style structure was created by architects Antonio Quintana Simonetti and Alberto Rodríguez using new technologies, like precast tunnels that formed sky bridges connecting the structures and vertical sun slides.

Because of its seafront location and lack of nearby buildings to protect it from the elements (until the Hotel Grand Aston went up in 2022), the structure has suffered the consequences of salt, wind and sun—but because the design was so well done, it stands determined to face all adversity, even the contempt of those who cannot appreciate its architectural attributes.

Some scenes from the Netflix series *Four Seasons in Havana*—written by Leonardo Padura (Reason #272) and starring Jorge Perugorría (Reason #257)— were shot here. [Malecón, btw E and F]

Cuban Napolitan

178 Star dishes at **Totò e Peppino**, named after two Italian comedians, include a five-layer homemade-pasta lasagna, melt-in-mouth eggplant Parmesan and a wood-oven *cornicione* pizza with prosciutto, buffalo mozzarella and fresh ricotta-stuffed crust. Hospitable owner Giselle Faedo Serrano, inspired by her Napolitano son-in-law Salvatore (Reason #127), keeps regulars devoted. [Calle 8, btw Calle 5 and Calzada; +535 250 3196]

From Italy with Love

179 **Café de la Esquina**, opened in 2017, is a well-run Italo-Cuban comfort food café. Pizzas on homemade dough are made on the spot and cooked in a refractory stone oven; fillings for thin calzone-like wraps, called *picos*, include traditional *ropa vieja* and fried sweet plantains. Refreshing Limonada Lizzie, frozen lemonade with *hierba buena*, is a fan favorite: it's on practically every table. Also, you can pop in for breakfast or an artisanal gelato. [Calle 5, Corner Paseo; +537 836 2565]

Luxury Trailblazer

180 The opulence of the past is reflected on Avenida Paseo, a grandiose boulevard with palatial homes and huge trees that shade you all the way from the Malecón to Plaza de la Revolución. This is the site of **Paseo 206**, a first-of-its-kind luxury boutique hotel, born through the passion and determination of visionary couple Andrea Gallina and Diana Sainz, who impeccably restored a 1930s colonial mansion to its original grandeur, turning out 10 lavish suites that radiate old-world charm with stylish mid-century furnishings and Marshall speakers. The only hotel in Cuba included in the Small Luxury Hotels of the World Collection, this is also home to a decadent, top-tier restaurant, **Eclectico**, serving up elevated Italian cuisine, exceptional espresso and spirited jazz nights; it's also open for breakfast. [Avenida Paseo 206, corner Línea; paseo206.com; +535 551 7894]

182

Malecón Wine Bar

181 **Costa Vino** is a dream made real by two Cuban sommeliers, Alejandro David Herrera Sarduy and Francisco Yoel Chacón Valdéz, who after a visit to Sonoma and Napa Valley decided to open up their own wine bar serving fresh seafood in 2019. Spanish wines alone take up a whole page on the wine list. [Calzada 1209, btw 18 and 20; +535 682 7292]

Yucca, Guava, Mango and More

182 Known by locals as **The Boutique**, this state-run *agropecuario*, (agro for short, or food market), is where many of the best chefs of Havana buy their produce. This place is your one-stop shop for whatever is in season—avocado, guanábana, chirimoya, mango, mamey... [Calle 19 and B]

183 B

184

Hubcap Hotel

183 Speeding right along, **Claxon** (A) is a boutique hotel fully decorated in a vintage automobile theme by owner Giselle Guerra Guerra, a huge fan of 1950s American cars. She went all out on her elegant, eclectic 2022 triumph with nine uniquely laid-out rooms, lush interior courtyard, rooftop terrace hosting weekly live jazz and car paraphernalia at every stop. The gourmet ground-floor restaurant is named **Fangio** (B) after the legendary Argentinian Formula 1 driver who has a very particular story with Cuba. Juan Manuel Fangio, one of the greatest race car drivers of all time, was kidnapped during the 1958 Havana Grand Prix by Castro's rebels, but took it coolly, which made him very popular among Cubans, who to this day identify with him, especially while driving. If someone is speeding, you may tell them, "Dale suave mi hermano, tu te piensas que eres Fangio?!" (Slow down bro, you think you're Fangio?!) [Avenida Paseo 458, btw 19 and 21; +535 095 6914; claxonhotel.com]

Vedado's Hidden Treasure

184 **Museo de Artes Decorativas** is one of my favorite museums in Havana. From the moment you walk in, everything is spectacular: the breathtaking view of the switchback staircase, the Carrara marble, and all that follows from rococo to art deco in this stunning mansion.

Designed in 1927 by French architects Virad and Destugue, it is the former home of José Gómez Mena—founder of the Manzana de Gómez shopping center, the first European style shopping mall in Cuba (now the Gran Hotel Manzana Kempinski; Reason #86)—who fled after the revolution, but not before hiding all his treasures in the basement. In 1964, it was turned into this museum of decorative arts with 33,000 pieces on display in its 11 original rooms.

Don't miss the gardens in the back, especially the Night Garden to the left. It has not been kept up as much as the sumptuous interior, making it somewhat surreal with its neoclassical sculptures. [Calle 17 #502, btw D and E]

Persian Delicacies

185 **Topoly** is an Iranian restaurant and shisha bar set in an enchanting mansion with a huge and inviting wraparound porch that makes for wonderful lounging.

Topoly—it means "big eater" in Persian—has a hefty menu of Iranian dishes specializing in lamb as well as vegetarian options like falafel sandwiches. Their pureed eggplant salad served with naan is bursting with flavors, and their cardamom tea with honey is soothing.

Its walls are covered with colorful portraits of iconic figures, including Charlie Chaplin, Ernest Hemingway, Mahatma Gandhi and Che Guevara, with famous quotes beside each figure. [Calle 23 #669, corner D; +537 832 3224]

Party All Night Long on Calle 23

186 **King Bar** (A) is best known for what is described as its "open-minded" atmosphere, hosting some of the wildest fiestas in town. The name King Bar is a play on the Cuban slang word *quimbar*, which means "to have sex." The atmosphere here is positive, upbeat and lively. Enjoy blaring pop and indie music late into the night and be ready for one of the best dance parties around. Retreat from the music and dancing to take a break on the large outdoor terrace. Weekend nights get packed quickly, so show up early or bring your patience! Open 10 p.m.-5:30 a.m. [Calle 23 #667 (enter via passageway), btw E and D; +535 196 6018]

The minute you walk into **EFE** (B), you take in the vibe of this styling and frenetic nightclub, featuring a mix of DJs and live music. Open 10 p.m.-6 a.m. [Calle 23 #605, corner F; +535 498 5791]

Another live music venue along Calle 23 with quirky artistic flair is **H_Bar** (C), featuring soul-stirring jazz soirées, flamenco and salsa as well as rum and cigar tasting. Open daily: 9 a.m.-3 a.m. [Calle 23 #461, between H and I; +535 475 4666]

Foodie Strip on Vedado's Malecón

187 Facing the Malecón, you'll find a glorious two-block stretch where you can feed almost any culinary desire. Stroll down Calle Primera (1ra) from the Meliã Cohiba (Reason #200) or the Hotel Riviera (Reason #203) and you'll run into **Beirut** (A) [Calle 1ra 237, btw A and B; +535 099 5044], where the naan bread is baked fresh daily, and the hummus, baba ghanoush and falafels do justice to the city it is named after.

For breakfast, pizza, a burger or delicious chicken salad, walk half a block toward the new Grand Aston Hotel to **Chuchería** (B) [Calle 1ra 107, btw C and D], which means "little treats," for comfort food, the closest thing to quality fast food in Havana and the best chocolate milkshake I've ever had.

Right next door and up the stairs for the elevated palette is **Casa Mia** (C) [Calle 1ra 103 btw C and D; +535 196 7544] or "my house." Three cousins saw their dream to fruition when they created a fine-dining establishment in the home they grew up in. Fish and mango ceviche, fried dumplings, octopus or beef carpaccio, lobster risotto, *ropa vieja* and an incredible tender fresh fish filet in creamy lemon sauce are just some of the options waiting for you. The maitre d' joked that the fish is so fresh it could have jumped over the Malecón seawall and landed on their stove.

188

All About Fidel

188 Fidel Castro's dying wish, to avoid the cult of personality, was for there to be no monuments or statues in his honor nor for any streets or squares to bear his name. **Centro Fidel Castro Ruz** is the single exception, as decreed by law. In 2021, on the fifth anniversary of Fidel's death, an astonishing grand-scale museum dedicated to his life and accomplishments was inaugurated in a 20th-century neoclassical mansion taking up an entire city block. The center is the country's most modern and interactive museum, with state-of-the-art touch displays meant to streamline the past for the new generation. The library was modeled on Hogwarts after a survey taken by kids on how they would like it to be. [Calle 11 #707, btw Paseo and Calle; +537 833 0292; centrofidel.cu]

187 C

Havana's Most Passionate Couple

189

This is the house in Havana that carries the most beautiful, tender and scandalous love story in the city. In the early 20th century, Catalina Lasa, a beautiful socialite, was married to the son of the vice president, but she fell madly in love with Juan Pedro Baró, a wealthy landowner. Catalina dared ask her husband for a divorce; he refused. Catalina and Juan Pedro fled to Paris and then to Rome to tell the Pope about their predicament. The Pope, so taken by the couple's intense love, blessed them and declared Catalina's marriage dissolved. They then married in Venice and returned to Havana where they were rejected by high society.

Juan Pedro constructed the most spectacular mansion for Catalina on Avenida Paseo, and during the five years of construction, the architects had to promise not to disclose the identity of the owners to the public. The secret would only be known 15 days before the inauguration in 1927, when Juan Pedro as vindication to Cuban aristocrats invited them all to marvel at his unique creation.

The elite were left speechless by the exceptional beauty of the neoclassical mansion—built by illustrious architects Govantes and Cabarrocas (who also designed the Xanadu Mansion (Reason #300) in Varadero, Dolce Dimora, now the Napoleon Museum, and the National Library)—and were especially awestruck by the sumptuous interior that was one of the first examples of art deco in Cuba.

The guests received artwork by local Cuban painters as parting gifts and accepted the couple back into society. But their happiness was fleeting, as Catalina became ill and died four years later. Her husband spent half a million pesos to build her final resting place, the most elegant and original art deco mausoleum in Cementerio de Cristóbal Colón (Reason #198).

Now run by the government, **Casa de la Amistad** (House of Friendship) is open to the public. You can visit the mansion and also have lunch or dinner in the grand dining room (Restaurante Primavera), the more casual outdoor terrace where you can catch a musical event or my absolute favorite spot, the Winter Garden, the gorgeous green room at the back with mind-blowing glasswork by René Lalique. [Paseo 406, btw 17 and 19; +537 833 8738]

Yoga: The Green Medicine of Cuba

190

Yoga bloomed in Havana after the decades-long effort of Cuba's universal yogi **Eduardo Pimentel**. President and founder of the Cuba Yoga Association in 1990, Pimentel began training in 1972, started teaching in 1982, was certified in Miami in 1992, founded **Estudio Vidya Yoga Cuba** in Havana in 1994, trained in India and Nepal in 1997, and joined forces with the International Association of Black Yoga Teachers in 1999 to develop a cultural yoga exchange between Cuba and the United States.

Eduardo has cultivated his own Cuban-style practice, implementing hands-on postural corrections that are appreciated by local yogis who are used to the extroverted qualities of the warm Latino people.

Until recently, the number of yoga practices in Havana was limited to a handful of instructors teaching out of their homes, but now, diverse yoga disciplines are offered across the city in private studios, at retreats and gyms, including Pura Vida (Reason #254).

Yoga was viewed by the revolutionary government as a religion throughout the 1980s, which impeded its growth until after the collapse of the Soviet Union in 1991. Then the government's view changed, and yoga was suddenly seen as "green medicine," an important anti-stress tool.

Eduardo continues to educate Cubans about the health benefits of yoga, including increased concentration, relaxation, stress relief, and general physical and mental well-being. He is known country-wide for his yoga broadcasts on national television. And his five inspiring books.

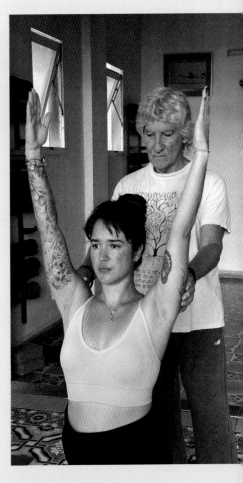

In the words of Eduardo: "Yoga is important for any society, but is special for us—yoga has been a kindness in difficult times."

Try one of Eduardo's classes at his studio on Saturdays: advanced at 8:30 a.m. and 9:45 a.m., intermediate at 11 a.m. and beginner at 12:15 p.m. Classes by Lisette, now co-director of the studio: Mondays 5:30 p.m. and Thursdays 5:30 p.m. [Calle 17 #813, apt. 2, btw Calle 2 and 4; +535 284 9737]

191

Cocktails and Cinephiles

191 When I asked Rafael Rosales, filmmaker and owner of **Café Madrigal**, what sets his bar apart, he said that his is a *coctelería con corazón*—a cocktail bar with heart. And what are the best cocktails? "All of them!" Open since 2011, this is Havana's first private bar since the revolution. With gorgeous high ceilings, exposed brick walls displaying movie memorabilia, and live music on weekends—jazz, bolero, nuevo trova , traditional son—Madrigal draws an artsy crowd of musicians, poets and film industry people, locals and tourists alike. Try to get a seat on the terrace and enjoy the light tapas menu of reinvented Cuban food nibbles. New to the space is their swanky cigar lounge with grand piano. [Calle 17 #809 (upstairs) btw 2 and 4; +535 826 4274]

Where to Stay in Style

192 With the influx of American tourists in 2014, *casas particulares* had to step up their game, and **La Reserva** (A) was one of the first to fill the high-end boutique hotel void. Boasting 11 meticulously planned rooms with exceptional taste in design, private en suite bathrooms, lush mattresses, Egyptian cotton linens...the offerings at La Reserva are arguably some of the best in Havana. Complete with an expansive tropical backyard patio for breakfast, dining and late-night drinks, their restaurant **La Bodega de la Reserva**, fuses Cuban and international flavors in what they call a "culinary laboratory." [Calle 2 #508, btw 21 and 23; +535 967 8521]

Literally next door is **Casa Brava** (B), which got its name from the bravura involved when Lorelis García De la Torre fearlessly renovated an eight-room Vedado mansion in complete disrepair, returning it to its former glory. Opened in 2017, they will make you will feel right at home here and especially blessed when lounging on the terrace with a book, for breakfast or apéro under the mango and avocado trees. [Calle 2 #510; +537 830 2665]

192A

Treasure Trove: Antique Shopping

193

Most tourists are unaware that antique shopping takes place in the private homes of Belkis and Ibrain, but ex-pats and diplomats alike scour these "shops" to find unthinkable hidden treasures from ages past. Be sure to bring your patience (and maybe a wet wipe or two) as you might have to get down and dirty to comb through layers of dust in order to find *your* treasure.

Bartering is a must at these places, though keep in mind that the owners most likely know much more about what they're selling you than you do! **Belkis** (A) [Calle 2 #607, btw 25 and 27] for crystal glassware, high-end vases, porcelain figures, furniture (don't forget to climb up the marble staircase for more gems). **Ibrain Portieles Torres** (B) [Calle 35 #251, btw 4 and 6] for 1950s chandeliers, lamps, clocks, furniture, including Bertoia chairs, Murano glass, vintage advertising signs.

193 B

Tribute Bar to the Fab Four

194

Just across from Parque John Lennon is **Submarino Amarillo** (A) (Yellow Submarine) [Calle 17, btw 4 and 6], a Beatles tribute bar that features amazing live cover bands. Opened in 2011, it was the first nightclub dedicated exclusively to rock 'n' roll in Havana. This music venue is so much fun because it is friendly and intimate with rock lovers, young and old, grooving to classics from all decades.

This colorful shrine to the Fab Four has Beatles memorabilia throughout the groovy decor with album covers, posters, lyrics and Blue Meanies on the walls, and a front facade painted like the cover of *Yellow Submarine*, with round windows, ring buoys and waves.

Get there early to grab a table and, if you dare, try their signature Submarino Amarillo cocktail made with rum, white wine, orange and pineapple juice, and a few drops of blue curaçao. They have a wide range of whiskeys as well, and you can order reasonably priced bottles of Havana Club rum to your table with cans of tuKola (local cola) to mix your own Cuba Libres.

You'll know you're at **La Casa de Bombilla Verde** (B) [Calle 11 #905, btw 6 and 8; +535 848 1331] when you see their namesake, an actual green lightbulb, hanging from the front porch rafters. It is a quirky, bohemian hipster hangout, where some of the best singer/songwriters in town like to gather and jam.

194A

Beatle Cast in Bronze

195 Fidel Castro declared a nationwide ban on Beatles music in 1964. He believed that they epitomized the decadent West. For decades, Cuban Beatles fans had to keep their appreciation for the music quiet. In time, however, Castro had a change of heart regarding his view of John Lennon—his crusade against war, racism and other forms of injustice led Castro to see him as a fellow revolutionary.

So on December 8, 2000, the 20th anniversary of Lennon's murder, **Parque John Lennon** was inaugurated when Castro unveiled a life-sized bronze sculpture of the former Beatle sitting on a bench while "All You Need Is Love" played in the background. At the foot of the statue is the inscription *Dirás que soy un soñador pero no soy el único*—"You may say I'm a dreamer, but I'm not the only one."

Have a seat on the bench with Lennon and, magically, an enterprising individual may conveniently appear to place round eyeglasses on the statue to momentarily replace the original bronze ones stolen from it, for your photo op. [btw Calle 6 and 8, and Calle 15 and 17]

Five-and-Dime

196 **Woolworth's** was a very successful American export to Havana, and three stores now called **Variedades** are still open—one on Obispo in Old Havana, one at Galiano and San Rafael in Centro Habana and another at Avenida 23 and Calle 10 in Vedado. Cubans called them *Ten Cent*, and they were much loved for their long counters where shoppers could pick out what they needed to buy with only mirrors on the pillars as security.

The Vedado store, still known as *Ten Cent*, has kept the Woolworth's logo embedded on the beautiful granite sidewalk in front. [Avenida 23, corner Calle 10]

197A

Cuban Institute of Cinematographic Art and Industry

197 Created in 1959, **Instituto Cubano de Arte e Industria Cinematográficos (ICAIC)** (A) [Calle 23 #1156, btw 10 and 12] is the state-run film production and distribution institution in charge of developing Cuba's film industry.

Walk into the lobby to see two mammoth 1930s movie projectors and a wall-to-wall—and ceiling—display of movie posters. It includes the explosion of 1960s pop art designs and all the Cuban classics, including *Fresa y Chocolate* (*Strawberry and Chocolate*)—the first Cuban production to be nominated for an Academy Award;

La Muerte de un Burócrata (*Death of a Bureaucrat*); and one of my personal favorites, *Soy Cuba* (*I Am Cuba*) by Mikhail Kalatozov, the poster illustrated by René Portocarrero (Reason #13). These classic images give you a pretty good idea of the evolution of post-revolutionary Cuba.

Afterward, go across the street to **Centro Cultural Cinematográfico Fresa y Chocolate** (B) [Calle 23 #1155, btw 10 and 12], a café and music venue where you may catch live bands on weekends. Or walk to the corner and check out **Galería Servando** (C) art gallery: named after renowned Cuban painter Servando Cabrera Moreno, it supports female artists and represents emerging Cuban artists from ISA (Reason #258). [Calle 23 #1151, corner 10]

have been answered have returned to place a plaque, flowers or a thank-you card, often with photos. The story goes like this: In 1901, Amelia Goyri and her baby died at childbirth and were buried together, with the child at the feet of the mother. When the coffin was exhumed several years later, they found the baby lying in the mother's arms.

You will see pilgrims and tourists alike practicing a ritual at the gravesite that developed because of Amelia's heartbroken husband. When she died, he began to visit the grave every day. He tapped the knocker on the tomb, and walked away backward so he could look at his loved one, frozen in time as a stoic Carrara marble statue, as long as possible.

Right next to Amelia you will see the art deco mausoleum of socialites Catalina Lasa and Juan Pedro Baró, Havana's most romantic couple (Reason #189). The tomb was designed by French glassmaker René Lalique. [Calle 12 and Zapata]

A Living Cemetery

198 You may think of cemeteries as morose, but along with being an inspiring tribute to some of Cuba's past inhabitants, **Cementerio de Cristóbal Colón** is also an awe-inspiring sculpture garden with fascinating design elements, and a place with an incredible history.

Built in 1876 and named after Christopher Columbus, this 140-acre necropolis is an absolute must-see. Since it would take a few days to see everything, get a map that shows the graves of some noteworthy artists, baseball players, politicians, writers, scientists and revolutionaries; the map is for sale near the Byzantine-Romanesque gateway, the Puerta de la Paz entrance.

Go see the grave of Amelia, La Milagrosa (The Miraculous One). Despairing or hopeful people from all over the world come to ask for her help to solve their life problems, or to fulfill their dreams. Some of those whose prayers

199B 199A

The Art Oasis

199 **José Emilio Fuentes Fonseca** (A), or JEFF, is an outstanding visual artist best known for his inflated metal elephant installation (pages 196-197), now at the Miramar Trade Center, that he inaugurated at the 2009 Havana Biennial by moving 12 of them from place to place in the city. Opened in 2022, his workshop/gallery and resto-bar, **Coco Blue y la Zorra Pelua** (B), is a space where art flows (literally: his sculptures lie all around the garden) and up-and-coming Cuban artists of all genres are featured. [Calle 14 #112, btw 11 and 13; +535 912 1916]

seen some of Cuba's best musicians take the stage in the 1950s Hard-Rock-Cafe-style setting, showcasing American wheels such as an old Chevy Bel Air convertible, a 1957 Buick, and a 1947 Harley Davidson—all under the watchful eye of a Soviet Yak-18 plane hanging overhead.

Make sure to check out their art gallery that displays the work of illustrious artists past and present, namely Esterio Segura, Frank Hart, Alfredo Sosabravo, Carlos Quintana, Remberto Ramirez and Marlys Fuego. And swing by their tobacco lounge on the 2nd floor, Casa del Habano. Even if you're not staying at the hotel, you can get a day pass to their expansive pool that sparkles invitingly under the warm sun. [Paseo 7, btw 1 and 3; +537 833 3636]

Meliãããã

200 Inspired by the Grand Prince Hotel Akasaka designed by Japanese architect Kenzo Tange, the Hotel **Meliã Cohiba** (A), built in 1994 right on the Malecón, was one of the first major hotel projects since the revolution. Constructed of Jaimanitas limestone to help protect against oxidation from the sea's salty assault, and with a redesigned lobby two meters over sea level to avoid flooding, this hotel has stood its ground as one of Havana's main business hotels.

On the entertainment side, their nightclub/cabaret **Habana Café** (B) has

200

Pathway to Good Food

202

Working as an architect, Maikel Paz decided to try his hand at something new. With a whole lot of love, he renovated a 1920s Vedado house, converting it into not only a stunning restaurant but also an inclusive and beloved gastronomic and musical hub. The name **paZillo** is a play on words—the restaurant's long narrow outdoor terrace is in the shape of a *pasillo* (passage), and the owner's name, Paz.

With incredibly fresh food supplemented by their outdoor garden, dreamy ceviche, *croquetas*, and rocking artisanal cocktails, know that it's also the best place to grab a decadent late-night burger. [Calle 5 #604, btw 4 and 6; +535 334 9570]

Their latest addition, around the corner, is paZillo Fresh, a great little grocery. [Calle 4, Centro Vasco, btw 3 and 5; +535 006 4513]

A Meal in a Mansion

201

Paving the way for other female entrepreneurs, like her head chef Zeida Chapman Menéndez, the innovative and soulful Niuris Higueras, owner and stand-in chef at **El Atelier**, loves to create dishes.

On a menu propelled by locally sourced produce and inspiration, you can find international and Cuban classics like local duck confit and a revisited *ropa vieja* dish, made with marinated lamb and seasoned to perfection.

Located in a Vedado mansion near the Meliã Cohiba hotel (Reason #200), this classy restaurant with spectacular service is consistently good. Check out the original wall art, including photographs by one of my faves Gabriel Bianchini: most of it is for sale. And don't miss the gorgeous balconies with ample room to lounge in style. [Calle 5 #511, btw Paseo and 2; +537 836 2025]

Nostalgia at The Riviera

203

When Mafia kingpin Meyer Lansky commissioned **Hotel Riviera** in 1957, the inspiration came from Las Vegas and his goal to out-do his Nevada mobster pals with a state-of-the-art casino and a swanky hotel that had it all. And he succeeded, until the 1959 revolution derailed his plans.

Stars like Ginger Rogers, William Holden, Nat King Cole and Ava Gardner were just some of the legends who stayed here. The hotel has survived six decades, and the vibe that goes with it remains intact. The Riviera is the place to go to relive the nostalgia of a bygone era.

The sleek, curvilinear architecture of the turquoise-hued facade captures the essence of 1950s modernism with clean lines and symmetrical design, making this, hands down, the masterpiece that melts my heart every time I lay eyes on it. The long white

203

marble lobby is timelessly elegant, as is the main bar with its large gold-plated wall mirror and original mid-century stage, set right behind the bartender. The retro charm of the pool out back with its legendary triple-tier diving board is the grand finale. [Paseo 1, corner Malecón]

203

English Books and Great Java

204 If you've satisfied your need for revolutionary history, take a stroll to English-language bookstore café **Cuba Libro**, a Local Development Project (PDL) founded by journalist and New Yorker by birth Conner Gorry. Featuring high-quality literature at very affordable prices, weekly trivia and other events, they also host book launches, readings and meditation classes. They are an LGBTQ+ safe space, with a robust cycling community and donation programs—they have surpassed 20,000 condoms distributed since opening in 2013. [Calle 24 #301, btw 19 and 21; +535 197 1567]

204

207

Unconventional Artist

206 Born in Argentina, **Enrique Rottenberg** spent his formative years in Israel, where he developed successful careers in real estate and filmmaking, but he chose to make Havana his home in 1993. Here, he continued his real-estate work, including development of the hugely successful Miramar Trade Center (Reason #250).

But his love of photography has been his main passion since 2007; he has risen to the top of the Havana art scene, while building up a following internationally. Rottenberg was the driving force behind the creation of the Fábrica de Arte Cubano (Reason #207), where his work is permanently on display. His art is smart, always provocative and sometimes controversial.

What are your origins? "My father is from Poland, my mom from Ukraine; I have a son and two granddaughters in Israel, a stepson who is Cuban-Russian in Havana, and another granddaughter who is American. I don't have a nationality. I am a citizen of the world. If there were a third world war, I wouldn't know where I would place my allegiance."

What do you love about Cuba? "Its people. The eye contact. They are very proud."

Describe your art. "I try to go to extremes and see how far I can go. I use nudity because clothes are a barrier between the soul of the subject and the photographer. But I always do this with the utmost respect and try not to humiliate. I make sure that it is not pornographic."

What is your favorite place in Havana? "My home."

Where do you feel best on the planet? "Company makes the place."

Dancing Under the Stars

205 Located at the very western tip of the Malecón, **Jardines del 1830** is a spectacular open-air nightclub. Set in the coral limestone garden of a beautiful old mansion, this is one of my favorite outdoor places to dance. From Friday to Sunday go to see the nimble locals gyrate, and you can also learn—or practice—your own moves all while dancing under the stars, right by the ocean. Never be shy to get up and dance; that's what Havana is all about! [Malecón 1252, corner Calle 22]

Factory of Fabulous

207

There is always a lineup around the block to enter this cultural hub and nightclub that has, since its inception in 2014, been the number one spot to be in Havana and possibly the world. Imagine a mix of Bauhaus and hot avant-garde Caribbean vibe, set in a number of galleries and performance spaces, all housed in a former cooking oil plant near the Río Almendares. Seen as the beacon of Havana's modern cultural revolution, **Fábrica de Arte Cubano** (FAC), created by legendary singer and composer X Alfonso, is visited by locals and foreigners, with trendsetters from all over the world arriving in droves, wanting to emulate this unique and groundbreaking experience.

It is so big you can get lost in this multimedia labyrinth that takes you step by step into a different dimension. Lounge, chill, think, drink, eat, meet people, shop, dance, watch movies, concerts and symphonies on top of the ever-changing art exhibits, or just hang out and let yourself be blown away by the place itself and the unexpected. [Calle 26, btw 11 and 13; open Thursday-Sunday, 8 p.m.-2 a.m.; fac.cu)

Tierra (Earth) is a culinary oasis within the crowd of about 2,500 that frequent the FAC daily: a clever strategy to avoid the inevitable lineup is to book a table at the restaurant, as it automatically gets you into the Fábrica.

The menu is designed to send you on a "trip around the world" as much as

208

provide a culinary art experience. Set in converted metal shipping containers, you can sit inside, with its atmosphere that feels like a comfortable country kitchen, or outside on the terrace with its Astroturf floor and funky bar, or up a level to the spectacular sky lounge. Whichever, you will find an enchanted sanctuary within a chaotic universe. [+535 565 2621]

Dining Under the Chimney

208 Attached to the FAC is **El Cocinero**, a gastronomic haven with the towering brick chimney marking the spot. The chic industrial feel of this fun rooftop lounge makes it one of Havana's essential restaurants. Open from noon until midnight every day of the week, they present perfectly prepared and presented mango daiquiris, avocado and tuna toast, fried plantains with *criollo* pork rillette and tempting blue cheese tart for dessert. While up there, make sure to climb the curved cast iron staircase and look up the chimney to see what's inside. [Calle 26 #57, btw 11 and 13; +535 842 0160]

207

PLAYA

Many seaside neighborhoods make up the municipality of Playa. Miramar, which means "look at the sea," is a posh green leafy residential neighborhood filled with creative *paladares*, live-music venues, outdoor nightclubs, theaters, the tropical Parque Almendares and Quinta Avenida, and the iconic boulevard and promenade that is the natural continuation of the Malecón. Buenavista is a village within a village, with vibrant culture, engaged locals and stunning street art.

In Náutico you can see Max Borges Jr.'s architectural arched masterpiece, in Cubanacán the unprecedented National Arts School, in Siboney sumptuous embassy residences, in the poor coastal fishing village of Jaimanitas entire blocks and homes covered with colorful tiles called Fusterlandia, and the Hemingway Marina in Santa Fé. Marianao is home to the legendary Cabaret Tropicana.

Marching Elephants by José Emilio Fuentes Fonseca (JEFF) (Reason #199)

240B
25

SANTA FÉ

1RA A
1RA C
158 A
3RA B
260

NÁUTICO

5TA AVENIDA

1RA
263
1RA AVENIDA

265B, C, D
JAIMANITA S
240A
150 A

265A
264
AVENIDA 3RA A
266

AVENIDA 3RA A
248
240
3RA C
5TA AVENIDA
188
5TA AVENIDA
17B
2

7MA
259

SIBONEY
CALLE 190
17A

13
15
17

CUBANACÁN

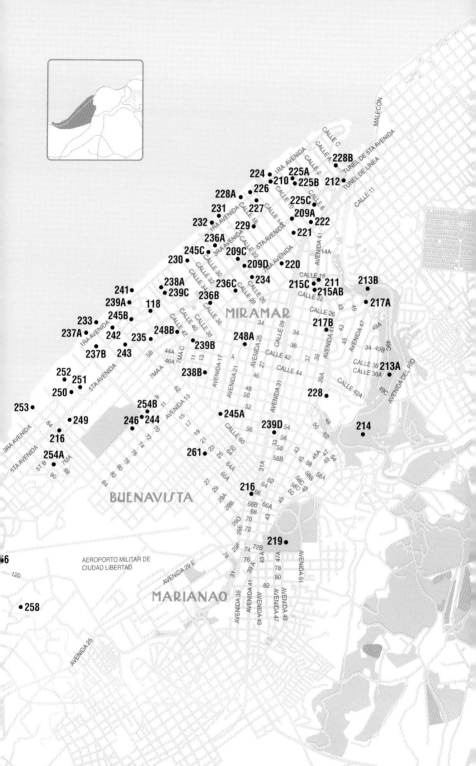

209 C

A Beautiful Drive and a Walk in the Park

209 Originally called Avenida de Las Americas—as you can see it inscribed on the 1924 white marble **Fuente de las Américas** (A) statue that immediately greets you when exiting the Río Almendares tunnel—**Quinta Avenida** (B) extends all the way to Río Santa Ana in the Santa Fé neighborhood. It takes 20 minutes to drive from one end to the other of this grand thoroughfare passing the many mansions and embassies that adorn the leafy upper-crust suburb.

The median strip of Quinta Avenida is a pedestrian path landscaped with manicured shrubs, flowers and trees and is frequented by joggers, cyclists, strollers and dreamers. You can't miss the clock tower at the corner of Calle 10 with its four bells emulating the sound of Big Ben in London.

Between Calle 24 and 26 are **Parque de los Ahorcados** (C) and **Parque Emiliano Zapata** (D). Split by Avenida 5, these parks share one of the most extraordinary, soulful and magical spots in all of Havana. Peaceful and romantic, with big beautiful banyan trees stealing the show, these enchanted parks are a blessed respite from any of your day's qualms. Sit on either side of Quinta Avenida and feel the splendor of the microclimate created in this singular spot. Nod to the statues of Mahatma Gandhi and Emiliano Zapata, the Mexican independence leader and staunch defender of the rights of Mexican Indigenous peoples and land reform.

A Splash of Eccentricity

210 **Rojo** is the wackiest resto/bar on this side of the Almendares River. Shoutout to Spanish owner DJ and showman Jorge Albi who brings his far-out vibes to the scene, expressing ideas through performances with musicians, dancers and actors. Order one of their signature cocktails—a Daft Punk or a Bad Bunny—and one of the best ceviches in town. [Avenida 1 #1002, corner Calle 10; +535 698 6390]

State-of-the-Art Mediterranean

211 One of Havana's pioneer innovative restaurants, **Otramanera**, opened by Spanish sommelier Alvaro Diez and his *habanera* wife Amy Torralbas, has been going strong since 2014.

Its succulent seasonal dishes include tuna tartare with avocado and mango, which you can pair, like I did, with a fresh strawberry daiquiri. Why not?!

The modern and sleek dining room is cool and inviting, setting the stage for a full-blown culinary experience. [Calle 35 #1810, btw 20 and 41; +537 203 8315]

Hidden Waterfront Restaurant

212 I love this cool little spot, ensconced around the bend from the Miramar tunnel. **Amigos del Mar** (Friends of the Sea) used to be a small fishermen's club before becoming this hip marine-themed *paladar* decked in sailing paraphernalia.

The outdoor multilayered terrace overlooks the mouth of Río Almendares with the smokestack of Fábrica de Arte Cubano (Reason #207) in full view. There is also a terrific bar that serves some of the most delicious mojitos in town. The staff is super-friendly, meals—go for the freshly caught lobster or the fabulous ceviche—are presented beautifully, and there is even a beached boat at the entrance that you can dine on. Sublime sunsets. [Calle Cero 511, btw Avenida 5A and 5B; +535 252 4887]

213A

A Trip to the Amazon in the Middle of Havana

213 **El Bosque de La Habana** (A) is the most spectacular natural wonder in Havana. The moment you enter this sanctuary of lush, greenery-drenched paradise you are in another dimension. Carob trees entangled by Tarzan-like vines plunge you into an enchanted urban jungle. Don't forget to breath in the fresh air of its unique microclimate that gives respite from the gas-fumed air of the city. El Bosque (The Forest) divides Vedado and Miramar, and is often called the lungs of Havana.

Within it you will find **Parque Almendares** (B), named after the river that flows through it. You will be amazed by the mammoth 300-year-old banyan trees covered in vines that look like big leafy green monsters. It's a great place to go for a walk or mountain bike along zigzagging paths by the river, take photos or visit the dinosaur park.

Don't be surprised if you see someone chanting and slitting the throat of a chicken and throwing it down the river, it is all part of a Santería ritual (Reason #281).

Alhambra à la Disney

214 This Cuban pleasure park with its exceptional neo-Moorish castle and quirky modernist landscape architecture is set in a jungle on the west bank of Río Almendares.

It was built in 1912 by the Blanco Herrera family, who owned La Tropical Brewery, the island's largest brewery at the time. Although time has taken its toll, **Los Jardines de la Tropical** is still a sight to behold. This multileveled wonderland with its exotic alfresco pavilion is the site for dance festivals and parties, and also a place to take a stroll and outlandish photographs. Buckle up for an unbelievable spectacle. [Calle Rizo, corner Avenida 51]

A Music Venue and Something Sweet

215 Set in a beautiful mansion, **Casa de La Música Miramar** (A) [Calle 20 #3308, corner 35] is a Havana institution. The country's best performers play into the night at this notorious nightclub that also hosts matinées, jam-packed with an authentic local crowd for steamy salsa and traditional music. Upstairs, the **Diablo Tún Tún Piano Bar** (B) serves up top-class acts, some of which a certain friend would not let me mention for fear word would get out! Equally emblematic is the swinging **Casa de La Música Habana** (Reason #134) in Centro Habana.

Directly across the street is a prized pastry shop, **Assukkar** (C) [Calle 20, btw 33 and 35], my go-to place for vanilla cake in a foot-long loaf, whole wheat bread (when flour permits), wine, champagne and even gin from Quebec.

214

215B

Craving Mexican?

216
Driven by cravings for Mexican flavors he couldn't find in Havana, Hector Veitia León devised his own solution: **La Catrina**, one of the tastiest restaurants in the city. The nixtamal quesadillas with fresh cheese and huitlacoche are stupendous. The guacamole, chilaquiles and pozole are beautifully plated but won't last long on your plate. His mother-in-law brings genuine Mexican skill to the corn tortillas she makes daily. Their Flor de Jamaica (hibiscus) lemonade frappé looks like a work of art and is the most delicious and refreshing I've had in the city. Warning: Hector claims that a weak cocktail can make you feel shortchanged, so he uses the more generous 60-ml jigger. Sit and sip Mexico's first beer, Carta Blanca, or a margarita while admiring the murals with skulls, roses and butterflies, and Frida Kahlo lookalike wait staff sporting floral crowns. [Calle 84 #503, btw Avenida 5ta and 5ta A; +535 659 3890]

Art Deco Charms

217
Havana is paradise for lovers of everything art deco; the city embraced the style in the early 1930s as the monumental Edificio Bacardí (Reason #84) went up in Old Havana and Edificio López Serrano in Vedado. But from the mid-1920s, art deco could already be appreciated in the interior design of Catalina Lasa and Juan Pedro Baró's mansion (Reason #189).

You will find art deco jewels scattered all across the city, including the **Salomón Kalmanowitz Residence** (A), a two-story house built in 1936 by architect Angel López Valladares. [Calle 28 #4517, btw 46 and 29]

During the early 20th century, Havana was ahead of its time; the city boasted as many movie theaters as New York or Paris. Among its beauties are Cine-Teatro Fausto, inaugurated on Paseo del Prado in 1938, Teatro América on Galiano in 1941 and others less-known, like **Cine Arenal** (B) that debuted in 1945. [Avenida 41, btw 30 and 34]

217 B

217 A

Wiwi's Wonderful Architectural Tours

218 Luis Eduardo González Díaz, who is known to friends as **Wiwi**, gives the most interesting and impassioned architectural tours of Havana. Wiwi finished top of his class at the Superior Technical Institute José Antonio Echeverría in 1984; he has 40 years' experience as an architect.

The affable Wiwi speaks impeccable English, has overflowing knowledge of the city, and is one of the kindest people I have ever met. His guided architectural tour could be one of the best things you do while in Havana. He offers a number of tours, but the best are the following:
- The five main squares of Old Havana (Colonial Period).
- Art deco Havana (1925 to 1935), including the Bacardí and López Serrano buildings.
- Modern Havana (1940 to 1964), a car tour in Vedado and Miramar.
- Jewish Havana: The Jewish Quarter and the city's synagogues.
- Cristóbal Colón (Christopher Columbus) Cemetery, renowned for its richness in art, history and marble sculptures.

[luiseduardogonzalezdiaz521@gmail.com; +535 838 9898]

Better than Vegas?

219 Havana's most popular nightclub and an institution since 1939, **Cabaret Tropicana** delivers one of the best shows out there. The costumes, the moves, the energy, the sensuality—you will be stunned. And so what if there are a lot of tourists, your eyes will be glued to the stage anyway.

The structure itself is also a sight to behold—a masterpiece by Cuban architect Max Borges Jr. (my idol!) with his telescopic parabolic vaults framing the setting.

I photographed backstage in 1995 while the performers were getting made up. Their friendliness and self-assuredness made for some sizzling shots as they seduced the camera like only a Cuban can.

The Tropicana was given a wink in Graham Greene's 1958 novel *Our Man In Havana,* and just as it was in its heyday, this exquisite, breathtaking and sexy show continues to impress. [Calle 72 #4504, btw 41 and 43; cabaret-tropicana.com]

Visual Artists to Keep an Eye On

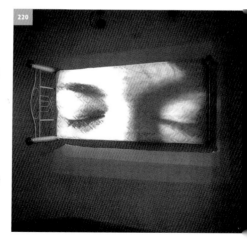

220 **Galería Artis 718**, which opened in 2014 to promote and sell Cuban art, features internationally renowned and emerging artists. Shoutout to: Rafael Villares, Adriana Arronte, Aluán Arguelles, Osy Milián, Duvier del Dago, Ernesto Fernández, José Manuel Fors, Luis E. Camejo and William Pérez among others. The gallery exhibits a diverse range of art forms. [Avenida 7, corner Calle 18]

Homemade Heaven

221 **Hecho en Casa** (Homemade) is such a cozy restaurant inside a small two-story house, where everything is fresh and the produce is meticulously chosen by Alina Menéndez Lamas, the chef-owner who has always sourced her food from artisanal farmers and organic butchers even before that was a thing.

Try the *ensaladilla Habana* (layers of tomatoes, goat cheese and basil), *frijoles rellollos* (I always go for black beans!), *picadillo de res* (mincemeat ground in-house), the pork fillet or fish of the day... And end off with the sorbet. [Calle 14 #511, btw Avenida 5 and 7; +537 202 5392]

Beer Drinkers and Art Lovers Unite!

222 **Espacios** in Miramar is set in a stunning mansion, with eclectic art by Cuba's most illustrious contemporary artists—including José Emilio Fuentes Fonseca (JEFF), Flora Fong, Ever Fonseca, KCHO, Eduardo Abela, Rafael Pérez Alonso and Karlos Pérez—on every inch of wall space.

In the back is a huge outdoor terrace where a sprawling green beer garden makes the perfect spot for an improvised fiesta. And this does happen here quite often, as popular musicians like Raúl Paz, Ray Fernández, Kelvis Ochoa, David Torrens and Big Bros, to name a few, drop by for spontaneous jam sessions at any given time.

With fluffy chickens running all over the place, you never know what you will experience, apart from the absolute certainty of fantastic food on your plate. Try my favorite pizza—arugula, fresh tomato and basil—straight out of the wood-burning oven, and their Tostones Javier (fried plantains topped with ceviche). And, if you dare, the Tobito, a nearly foot-tall mojito named after legend Toby Brocklehurst (Reason #251). [Calle 10 #513, btw Avenida 5 and 7; +535 266 3133]

A Gentle Giant of Afro-Cuban Art

223 The only other person I have ever met that exudes peace and love like the Dalai Lama is **Manuel Mendive Hoyo**. Born in 1944, he is considered by many to be the most important Cuban artist living today.

Mendive is a gentle soul, diametrically opposed to the explosive nature of his work that explores Afro-Cuban history, the Santería religion and mythology through richly hued paintings, sculpture and performance.

As we spent the morning together, swaying on a loveseat swing at his quaint countryside residence, he talked of faith, love and believing in the power of good over evil. As he gazed onto the valley of royal palms, the sky and its changing colors and shapes of the clouds, contemplating Nature, his muse, his words kept echoing back: focus on the positive and find beauty in everything. It was the answer to every question.

His home, studio and private gallery are set in a lush pocket of nature in the countryside of Mayabeque, the nearest province east of Havana. Climbing up an outdoor hand-laid stone stairway to his private gallery was like stepping into a world where everything is bursting with energy and meaning. I got to view his paintings and sculptures, which seem to manifest the powerful emotions veiled by his quiet presence.

Mendive graduated from the distinguished Academia Nacional de Bellas Artes San Alejandro and his art resides in museums and galleries worldwide, including Finland, Congo, Jamaica, and the United States.

Karl Marx Theater

224

With a capacity of 5,000, **Teatro Karl Marx** is Havana's largest indoor performance space. When it was built in 1949, it was Cuba's largest cinema, known as Teatro Blanquita.

Today, it operates as a live theater and concert venue, where a blend of Cuba's standout musicians from both the present and the past have performed, including Silvio Rodríguez, Pablo Milanés, Carlos Varela and X-Alfonso. The theater has also hosted the best comedy acts in the city, like that of Pánfilo, the celebrity comedian who did a skit playing dominos with then-President Barack Obama during his 2016 visit. [Avenida 1, btw 8 and 10]

Walter's Angels

225

Nero di Seppia (A) [Calle 6 #122, btw Avenida 1 and 3; +535 478 7871] is one of the best Italian restaurants in Havana; it serves perfect wood-burning stove pizza, homemade pasta and immense fresh salads.

Italian chef-owner Walter Ginevri, with his wide sparkling smile and stunning all-female staff, will make you feel right at home. Try their tremendous *tagliata* (sliced steak), spicy diablo pizza and the taco chicken salad; be sure to end on a sweet note with their melt-in-your-mouth guava cheesecake and one of the finest espressos in the city. Sit on the terrace for lunch or dinner and get spoiled.

Right next door is **Toros y Tapas** (B) [Calle 6 #124 btw Avenida 1 and 3; +537 202 1548] for a trip to Spain. Try their flawless traditional tortilla or the paella that pairs perfectly with abundant Spanish wine options and don't think about leaving before tasting the chocolate lava cake.

Roll out the red carpet and walk up to the classiest act in town, **Boutique Hotel Casa Italia** (C), a 19-room luxurious boutique hotel and restaurant, featuring a Florentine chef making waves with his phenomenal food, all perfectly paired with an enviable wine list selection. Try the savory pecorino cheese and pear ravioli with truffle sauce, caramelized pork steak or the perfect pizza from their exquisite wood-fired oven covered in golden ceramic specially imported for the restaurant from Naples. [Calle 6, btw Avenida 5 and 5A; +535 216 9927]

Seven Days of Seaside Sunsets

226 Located on the beachfront, **7 Días** is a prime spot to watch the sunset, drink in hand while munching on homemade banana chips for starters. This well-run restaurant with attentive staff is open every day of the week as indicated by their name, "7 Days."

From their meticulously landscaped outdoor terrace, you can take in the scene at the public beach: local teens flirting or couples sitting on concrete partitions drinking rum as the sun reaches the water's edge on the horizon. [Calle 14 #1402, corner Mar; +537 209 6889]

A Very Special Place to Dine

227 In 1995, Hubert and Manolo opened a unique *paladar* in their exquisite art deco home once owned by a woman they loved very much named Esperanza. They kept her spirit alive by displaying her portrait, her memorabilia, the original furnishings and by christening it **La Esperanza**.

Come for an intimate dining experience in the comfort of a 1920s house containing extensive creative ornamentation that gives the space a sensual sexy wonderland feel. There is a full-on living room with a cozy sofa, and chairs where you can enjoy drinks before or after dinner, a luxuriant outdoor patio, and fresh-cut flowers on every table.

You have to try the most bizarre dish I've ever had—the *Banana de Ochún*, a plantain covered with tuna, cheese, red wine, honey, cinnamon and hot sauce that was actually very good! Or the delicious chicken curry and their *Pollo Luna de Miel* (Honeymoon Chicken) in honey sauce flambéed with Cuban rum.

I once bumped into Jamie-Lee Curtis, who clearly loved the place as much as I did. [Calle 16 #105, btw Avenida 1 and 3; +535 281 0461]

Party on the Cutting Edge

228 Dance along the coast to titillating cutting-edge Cuban fusion at **Don Cangrejo** (A). The live music at this alfresco seaside nightclub rocks. Especially on a Friday night! Doors open at 10 p.m., so get there early to beat the lineup. [Avenida 1 #1606, btw 16 and 18]

To extend the revelry, walk over to **Johnny Club (El Johnny)** (B), one of the oldest nightclubs in Havana, that in 1959 was well-frequented by the upper crust. Transformed with cutting-edge tech in 2022, this is a next-gen mega party haven. [Calle A, btw Avenida 3 and 5]

State-Run Flamenco Rock

229 The tocororo is the national bird of Cuba, and it is unique to the island. **Tocororo** is also the name of a classic state-run bar and live music venue that has standout bands and singers every night and I especially like to go for the always fun "flamenco-rock" band, complete with flamenco dancers. A DJ usually takes over afterward, and only stops playing tunes when the guests stop dancing.

Pro bar staff mix cocktails at the old American-style bar serving ham and cheese plates, and other snacks to nibble on. If you go as part of a group, you can be economical and buy a bottle of rum, vodka, whiskey or gin and mixers, and make your own drinks at your table.

The outdoor terrace is the perfect spot for a relaxing aperitif or nightcap. [Calle 18, corner Avenida 3]

Seaside Feasting

230 Sipping a fresh passion fruit daiquiri to the sound of the waves hitting the seawall as the dramatic Havana sunset takes my breath away once again, I realize I'm at one of the most romantic dinner spots in Havana. **Arrecife** (Coral reef) is perched along the coast in Miramar. Amazing appetizers include paper-thin sashimi, smoked salmon sushi and my favorite, fish croquettes, made with classic Bechamel, heavy on freshly grated nutmeg. [Calle 32, btw Avenida 1 and Mar; +535 614 6377]

Ocean Breeze

231 Providing an unparalleled backdrop of infinite pink and orange sunsets reflected in their infinity pool, combined with crashing waves on the seawall, this opulent yet simple setting amazes. Welcome to **Vistamar**, one of the oldest *paladares* in the city, opened in 1996 by the Riva family who have always maintained highly professional, knowledgeable and friendly staff. My family and I swear by the shrimp tacos, confit octopus, grilled snapper and curry chicken. When we are there with our friend Nathali Soave, we always order the Soave wine, but the Ribera del Duero is also delicious and their fresh pineapple juice reigns supreme. [Avenida 1 #2206, btw 22 and 24; +535 013 6525]

Antiques Café

232 **Café Fortuna** was named because of the good fortune the owner, a designer, had at getting this ideal spot. Joel already had a collection of antique paraphernalia, but his friends kept adding to it and the expanded collection helped make the café one of a kind. Wait until you see the mini museum of all things retro and old, including an 18th-century carriage transformed into a booth. The café is like a fantasyland, and guests play the part when Joel throws theme parties, like hippie night, a vampire festival, or his Halloween blowouts.

The all-male staff, in marine-themed striped white-and-blue shirts and sailor's caps, serve up omelets in the morning and sandwiches and homemade snacks throughout the day and evening. Open until midnight, their signature cocktails include the Vampisol; a mixture of red wine, whiskey, orange juice and lime rind that once consumed is meant to enable vampires to endure sunlight... [Avenida 1, corner 24]

Just B-r-e-a-t-h-e

233 **Michel Uranga Briñas** is my go-to Kundalini instructor in Havana. Once a week we unroll our yoga mats on the Havana coastline and spend an hour breathing deeply and searching deeply inside ourselves, while the sea rolls out its daily flow. We end with a dip in the crystal-clear water and...instant bliss: the day could not begin in a better way.

Michel started out as a Thai masseur before receiving certification for Hatha yoga in the U.S. and Kundalini yoga in Mexico. He created **Agata Yoga** in 2018 to instruct and enlighten the growing community of yogis in Cuba. Michel has formed a dream team that teaches Ayurveda, astrology, massage therapy and yoga. He finds that Kundalini yoga in particular best bonds body, mind and soul, and that it gives the maximum amount of benefits in the shortest amount of time.

"Your emotions are nothing more than the chemicals of your respiratory pattern," he said. "If you learn to breathe more consciously, you will be able to balance your mind—and control your emotions." [Contact Michel by phone or WhatsApp for class schedule and spiritual retreats; +535 265 6874]

Roast Chicken Legacy

234 **El Aljibe**'s roast chicken was long the most iconic in the city, and their celebrated BBQ sauce recipe still remains top secret. The abundance of side dishes, including sweet potato chips, salad, savory black beans and rice that the very efficient wait staff scoop onto your plate, make a trip to this institution a special treat. Worth noting: El Aljibe also has an excellent cigar shop. [Avenida 7, btw 24 and 26; +535 324 7017]

Comfort Food Boom

235 This spacious, indoor/outdoor restaurant is decorated in a Betty Boop theme and even though they mispronounce her name, Betty is everywhere—down to the cheery waitress' pert outfits. **Betty Boom** is known for its massive fresh salads, pizzas, burgers and quality grilled meats from the open-air kitchen, and is fully equipped with a playground to keep the kids entertained. [Avenida 5ta, at Calle 60; +535 916 3757]

The Calmest Spot and a Beauty Frenzy

236

You got to love **Luly Salón** (A), with the long row of mani-pedi stations, complete with fancy glass basins for your feet where you can get your hair blow-dried at the same time. And order a drink, salad or coffee all while chatting with the Cuban *farándula*, or expat community. [Calle 26 #120, 2nd floor, corner Avenida 3; +537 206 5859]

The place to go in Miramar for a facial and massage in a pristine and serene setting is **VidaSpa** (B). They use products with 100% natural ingredients and their attentive care will take you to a stress-free universe. [Calle 34 #308, btw Avenida 3 and 5; +537 209 2022]

Two blocks from VidaSpa, but a galaxy away, is **Belleza Latina** (C), the colorful, happening labyrinthine spa that is abuzz with Cuban beauties sitting pretty for a plethora of treatments and hairdos. They also have a spinning gym in the back and a small café up front. [Calle 30 #319, btw Avenida 3 and 5; +537 205 5411]

Maritime Mishmash

237

Paseo Marítimo (aka **1ra y 70** (A) was an abandoned stretch of coastline until 2020 when the government allowed private businesses onto the land. Today there are a dozen or so restaurants resembling large beach shacks, a playground for kids, including a trampoline and electric bull, and tiki umbrellas all along the shore. Everything under the sun can be found: sushi with a Michelada, tapas and Hawaiian-themed cocktails, seafood pizza and beer on tap. It is one of my favorite sunset spots. You can't miss it just beside MGM's **Grand Muthu Habana** (B) hotel. [Avenida 1ra, btw 60 and 70]

Heightened Cuisine

238

Ingenious chef **Enrique Suárez** has traveled the world, learning from the culinary greats, yet it all began in his childhood home where he taught himself how to cook at just nine years old. After opening **TocaMadera** (A) Knock on Wood in 2016 in an unpretentious space in upscale Miramar, he took Havana by storm spearheading an exciting culinary revolution. This restaurant is sacred to my family, we are equally enamored by Enrique as we are addicted to the dishes. Truffle risotto, tostones, torched tuna, ceviche, crispy vegetable nigiri, the brownie...this is too good to miss!

How did you learn to cook? I used to cook for family and friends because I come from a family of good cooks. My grandmothers are queens in the kitchen! My father's side was wealthy; my mother's side was very poor, but all of them were able to make amazing dishes, full of flavor.

One day, a friend encouraged me to sell my food, and it was a success. I then started a self-learning process, in search of a different cuisine—something more interesting and diverse. As a result, I was invited by a Michelin Guide writer to cook at six restaurants in France. The following summer, I was in the kitchens of the renowned Sagardi Group, an international Basque restaurant project in Barcelona. I also had a remarkable opportunity in Marseille, in a Mediterranean restaurant owned by Marcel Dib, who once played soccer for the French national team. The learning tour was completed after I cooked for 70 at IFTM Top Resa, a tourism industry trade fair, in Paris. All of these experiences really made a difference.

The concept? Poor-people cuisine, strong flavors and recycled design. I'm trying to do something interesting, putting together our traditional food with modern flavors. It's really about giving poor-people cuisine—and the people who made it—the credit deserved for inspiring the good food that we have around the world today. Our Cuban forefathers had to rely on scraps and make magic to put a good meal on the table.

The art on the walls? Manuel Mendive Hoyo (Reason #223), Cirenaica Moreira and Enrique Ávila.

The produce? Fernando Funes (Reason #293), who is a farmer with a PhD in agronomical sciences, supplies us with some of the best produce on the island; his organic farm project is 12 miles (20 kilometers) west of Havana.

238A

WALL OF FAME: Enrique Suárez has cooked for Enrique Iglesias, Carolina de Monaco, François Hollande, Oliver Stone, Susan Sarandon, Danny Glover, Owen Wilson, Michael Voltaggio, Kailash Satyarthi, Piedad Córdoba, La Bella Cubana, and Graziano Pellè.

The drinks? Watermelon daiquiri, blueberry vodka tonic, grapefruit juice mojitos with ginger, mango martini. [Calle 38 #118, btw Avenida 1 and 3; +535 281 2144]

Care to share a taste of what's to come? I am a chef and partner in the newly reopened **La Cocina de Lilliam** (B) [Calle 48 #1311, btw 13 and 15; +535 080 1217], one of the first and most iconic *paladares* in Havana opened in 1994.

Our goal is to showcase the culinary fusion born from the diverse cultures found in Cuba, including Indigenous, Spanish, African, Asian, Italian and French influences.

238A

Homemade Ice Cream

239

Beat the heat with artisanal ice cream in a huge variety of flavors that you can enjoy on the ample outdoor terrace at **El Gelato** (A). Tiramisu, dark chocolate, *guanábana* or plain frozen yogurt are all scoops I opt for. Open every day from 7 a.m. until midnight, they serve fresh breakfasts from their outdoor kitchen, donuts, outlandish cakes, croissant sandwiches, but sometimes I just like to stop by after yoga on the coast nearby for ice cream and espresso to start the day...*¿por qué no?* [Avenida 1 #4215, corner Calle 46]

Havana ice cream queen and **Café Enlace** (B) owner Irina Sotolongo doles out 100% organic gelato that she started out making and selling from her garage to the international community and luxury restaurants. Get ready to try the *Flor de Jamaica* (hibiscus), *maracuya* (passion fruit,) dehydrated pineapple, chocolate, rum and tobacco, avocado (!) and wait for it...curry gelato. [Calle 42 #910, btw Avenida 9 and 11]

Ambrosía (C), "the food of gods" in Greek, opened in 2023 when Tony Loiacono began importing Italian soft-serve: it is one of the most sublime sensations on a hot Havana day. Their coffee and plain frozen yogurt that you can order at a stand in front are angelic. They serve waffles and tea plus other treats on their outdoor patio. [3ra #3804, btw 38 and 40; +535 296 6566]

You won't miss **Lola Café** (D) if you look for a giant plexiglass poppy outside, an iconic work by Lucia Zalbidea. This small bakery has a plethora of pastries like guava tarts and brownies but also ice cream calling your name, like coconut, peanut butter and condensed milk. [Calle 31 #5409, btw 54 and 56]; **Dolce Neve** (E) dazzles with brain-freezing moundfuls of gelato and Neapolitan pastries. [Avenida 1, corner 36]

239A

240 A

The Sport that Cubans Invented

240

Cubans do a lot of things their own way—*a lo cubano*—and **cancha** (A) is one of them. Cancha is a racket sport with two to four players competing within a three-wall court, using tennis rackets and a racquetball—preferably a pink one to contrast with the green walls.

Created in the 1940s, cancha has been going strong despite lack of funds to invest in resurfacing old courts and building new ones. The court is 65 feet (20 meters) long and 23 feet (7 meters) both wide and high. Although baseball, boxing and basketball are Cuba's most popular sports, cancha is the only one unique to the island and it's played nationally with hard-fought championship matches.

Pack your tennis racket and head to any public cancha court in search of a game. You might have to wait in line (*la cola*), but that is how you make friends in Cuba,

with patience and humor. Club Havana (Reason #263) has both cancha and tennis courts.

Paddleboard or windsurf along the Havana coastline with instructor Alejandro Frómeta Gómez of **SUP in Cuba** (B). [Avenida 3ra and Calle 112 (walk west along the coast through parking lot on Calle 110 to La Concha beach); +535 196 9769]

Scuba dive with Javier Torres of **Dive Adventure Havana**. [+535 293 8619]

240 B

241

Brazilian-Themed Poolside Paradise

241 On a piping hot Havana day, make a beeline to the large and picturesque pool at **Hotel Copacabana** located directly on the coast overlooking the sea.

Their popular poolside bar with barstools in the water provides sunbathers with food and drink. There is even an original saltwater pool sunken into the ocean so you can swim "in the sea" without worrying about the coral that lines the Havana seaside. The pool attracts a nice mix of locals and tourists (small fee if you are not a hotel guest). [Avenida 1 #4404, btw 44 and 46]

Catch a Dolphin Show

242 The dolphin show at the **Acuario Nacional** is really well done and is as fun for adults as for kids. One show involving three human divers is completely underwater, seen through glass. Without breathing equipment, they perform intricate acrobatics with the dolphins. Another one seen from the stands has three dolphins synchronized jiving to Latin music. The aquarium doubles as an educational facility and science center, specializing in marine research and environmental awareness and protection.

Fidel Castro enjoyed bringing guests to see the dolphins; he called them "very intelligent animals." [Avenida 1, btw 60 and 62]

242

Ideological Architecture

243

You can tell that the whopping 20-story **Russian Embassy** tower was built during the heyday of Soviet-Cuban friendship, before the collapse of the Soviet Union in 1991 and the withdrawal of comradely support.

Though I may be in the minority, I love this 1980s concrete and glass brutalist building by eminent architect Alexander Rochegov, who subsequently became president of the Russian Academy of Architects.

It is known by many names, some of them unmentionable in public, but I particularly find fitting the comparison to a plunging sword—it makes me think of the Arthurian legend of Excalibur, a sword that only a true king could pull from a stone. Maybe it was a wink to their old buddy, Fidel Castro? [Avenida 5 #6402, btw Calle 62 and 66]

243

244

A Sensational Stop

244

Watch your spaghetti carbonara being mixed with freshly grated cheese in a giant Parmesan wheel, or Caesar salad tossed at the table like in the 1920s, at tasty **Sensaciones**. Savor fresh burrata cheese, beef tenderloin, mushroom risotto or shrimp tacos in purple corn tortillas, which are my favorite in town. For dessert try the *quesillo de coco* (coconut flan) or the *torrijas en almíbar* (simply French toast with syrup). A variety of rooms and environments accommodate every mood: I always choose the upstairs terrace that faces right onto Parque Monte Barreto. [Calle 70 #902, btw Avenida 9 and 11; +537 206 1831]

245 B

No-Name Flower Market

245 There is a pretty little **flower market** (A) made up of vendors who operate in the front yards of their tiny homes on a tree-lined street. Romantics of all kinds whip in and out of these stands using all modes of transport—bicycles, motorcycles, trucks, cars—and continue on their way with armfuls of color and beauty. A large bouquet of fresh-cut seasonal flowers is a steal. [Calle 60, btw Avenida 19 and 21]

For exotic plants at rock-bottom prices, visit Antonio the great at my favorite *vivero* (nursery)(B). [Calle 60, corner Avenida 3]

For all-natural enthusiasts, the tiny sustainable green grocery store **Verde Verde** creates their own line of organic goods and collaborates with small Cuban businesses that share their values, showcasing an array of locally sourced products—homemade pesto, peanut butter, goat cheese, artisanal bread, and naturally farmed vegetables from Finca Marta (Reason #293) [Calle 3 #2804, btw 28 and 30; +535 241 3678]

Superstar Italian Feast

246 **La Corte del Príncipe** has seen the likes of visiting celebrities, including Madonna, Katy Perry and the Rolling Stones, all displayed on the wall in frames posing with owner Sergio, a "rockstar" in his own right who died a few years ago.

The casual alfresco terrace is the setting for a homemade Italian feast—the *parmigiana di melanzane* (eggplant Parmesan) appetizer is one of the tastiest things I've ever eaten: it melts in your mouth. I dream about this dish. And I never go there without ordering the *tagliatelle ai funghi porcini* (tagliatelle with porcini mushrooms) and the shrimp with avocado (when in season). [Avenida 9, corner 74; +535 255 9091]

246

The Golden Age of Cuban Rum Is Now

247 This Caribbean island that I call my second home is the home of rum. Its predecessor, "tafia," was a raw and intense spirit based on sugarcane molasses that pirates and privateers chugged down until light rum was created in the mid-1800s by Facundo Bacadrí of Santiago de Cuba, who founded the island's first distillery. He developed a short fermentation process that produced smoothness and clarity, and suddenly this light rum became the go-to drink of the upper class.

It was Cuba's financial savior in the 1990s when the USSR collapsed and foreign aid dried up. Pernod Ricard formed a joint venture with Cuba Ron to export Havana Club all around the world. It was the first of a series of partnerships that revolutionized the industry, with Cuba leading the way in rum-making excellence.

Today, rum is gaining recognition as a digestif rivalling whiskies and cognacs, with new types of premium quality rum that use traditional production methods. As a recognition of the expertise of generations of Cuban rum masters—beginning with the first Maestro del Ron Cubano, legend **Pedro Pablo Navarro Campa**—UNESCO declared Cuban Rum Masters' Knowledge as Cultural Heritage in 2022.

The youngest of a select group of just nine Cuban Rum Masters in the country, and trained by Campa himself, Cesar Martí told me that rum is the symbol of Cuba: joyful, multicolored, hospitable and selflessly friendly. It has been a faithful companion of the people in moments of joy and celebration, but also in moments of sadness and pain, across all social sectors: from *macheteros* (cane cutters) to aristocrats. The culture around rum is about giving, even though Cubans don't have much.

Two of the newest rums for you to try: Eminente, Cuba's premium rum created jointly by Moët Hennessy and Cuban government entity Cuba Ron with Cesar Martí, and promoted by former film director, actor and rum aficionado Raúl Bravo because "Eminente respected the culture and values of my country. Cuba Ron has a beautiful legacy."

On the market since 2019, Black Tears is the first Cuban spiced rum. "Cubans are not traditionally spiced rum drinkers, but they are catching on," says company president Enrique Bernardo Arias. The rum is named after a famous Cuban song "Lágrimas Negras," about a woman who cries many black tears of sorrow over a lost love into a barrel of rum, giving it a deep flavour.

Party Until the Sun Shines

248

A fun place for late night drinks and dancing is **SangriLa** (A) —a sociable spot where a stranger may start salsa dancing with you the moment you walk in. [Avenida 21, corner Calle 42]

And after ShangriLa, everyone heads to **Mio & Tuyo** (B) for a nightcap... or until 6 a.m. [Avenida 5b, btw 42 and 44; +535 289 3625]

248 B

Landmark Catholic Church on 5th Avenue

249

Completed in 1953, the beautiful and colossal neo-Romanesque **Iglesia de Jésus de Miramar**—with its giant dome—is Cuba's second-largest church.

It houses Cuba's largest pipe organ (5,000 pipes) and gorgeous murals of the stations of the cross by Spanish artist Cesareo Hombrados Oñativia. The painter used his wife as model for the Virgin Mary, and many of the colorful crowd scenes include the faces of those who sponsored the project.

Walk in the gardens of the church grounds to see a replica of the grotto of Our Lady of Lourdes, designed by eminent architect Max Borges Jr. There is a huge abandoned green field in the back, where I like to photograph the church from a distance, hardly able to imagine that Quinta Avenida, one of Havana's busiest thoroughfares, is just on the other side. [Avenida 5, corner Calle 82]

High-End Tailor-Made Trips to Havana

251 Toby Brocklehurst, a British native who has been working in Havana for 30 years, is your man in Havana for a customized trip of the city through his high-end tourist and concierge service, **In Cloud 9**.

Being well-connected, and with his encyclopedic knowledge of the country, Toby can make just about anything happen: a private dinner in a mansion with renowned Cuban musicians, an exclusive visit to a tobacco plantation with cigar experts, engaging architectural tours, one-of-a-kind diving excursions and tailored getaways to anywhere on the island. In Cloud 9 also specializes in high-end property rentals and film production. A unique experience is guaranteed. [info@incloud9.com]

The Amazing Israeli-Cuban Joint Venture

250 A brainchild of Enrique Rottenberg (Reason #206), **Miramar Trade Center** is an office building complex and retail space that went up in 2000 and now includes six buildings: Jerusalem, Barcelona, Habana, Santiago, Santa Clara and Beijing. It houses offices, restaurants, travel agencies, ETECSA (the state-run telephone company), and a wine shop and bar, among other enterprises.

Check out the charming herd of **inflated metal elephants** (see page 196), created by Cuban Artist José Emilio Fuentes Fonseca (JEFF) (Reason #199), displayed during the 10th Havana Biennale and now trundling along Avenida 3 between Calle 70 and 80.

Executive Hotel with Gastronomic Flair

252 The **Meliã Habana** is a huge business hotel complex with a bunch of restaurants, including **Plaza Costa Habana**, first-of-its-kind food trucks serving high-end street food in their inner courtyard; Japanese-style; La Bella Cubana a savory Italian La Scala; the Titanium Sports Bar, plastered with flat-screen TVs; an executive VIP buffet on the ninth floor for power breakfasts; and the Robaina cigar lounge and shop, where you can find high-grade hand-rolled cigars, drink coffee or cocktails and speak to the cigar sommelier. They also have Havana's largest pool, which stretches along the coast. [Avenida 3, btw Calle 76 and 80; +537 204 8500]

The Commodore and More

253 Built during the heyday of Mafia-backed hotels in the 1950s, the then five-star **Hotel Comodoro** was said to be one of the most luxurious on the island. It was built on the seawall with a magnitude of installations and services in a style that can only be described as modern.

Today, the hotel is part of a sprawling complex of bungalows, Venetian-style canals and bridges, 10 pools including a natural sea water basin, a shopping center, supermarket, beauty salon, pub with outdoor seating, steakhouse including artsy cigar lounge and a first-class cigar store with excellent staff.

Interestingly, the hotel had a post-revolutionary hiatus when it was turned into a school for art instructors trained in music, dance, theater and drama who, upon graduation, were dispersed across the island as cultural emissaries.

The vintage car club (Reason #162) meets here on Saturdays at 3 p.m. A must-see! [Avenida 3, corner Calle 84]

From Exertion to Euphoria

254

Pura Vida (A) is a fitness center with health practitioners who endorse a complete mind-body concept with a modern gym that offers personalized training, boxing classes, yoga, Pilates, Zumba, meditation, TRX and TRX for kids! They also boast 15 types of massages, facials and an energizing café for fresh salads, sandwiches, natural fruit smoothies, oatmeal cookies, and lemon and banana bread. [Calle 88 #525, btw Avenida 5 C and 7; +537 209 4634]

To pump iron with Cuban *farándula*, go to **Club 905** (B). [Calle 70 #905, btw Avenida 9 and 11].

Legendary Passion Under the Big Top

255

Circus acts have performed in Cuba for more than 200 years; the performers themselves were, and continue to be, revered almost as much as baseball players, which says a lot.

Circo Trompoloco is the place to enjoy these talented and award-winning acrobats, contortionists, strongmen and hyperactive clowns every weekend. The circus is located in the huge red-and-white tent near the entrance to La Isla del Coco Amusement Park, formerly called Coney Island. While the equipment may be archaic, the talent is fresh, so come be bedazzled by some of the world's best acts. [Calle 112, btw Avenida 3 and 5]

Inspiration Beyond Borders

256

Alexis Leiva Machado, aka **KCHO**, is an internationally acclaimed, award winning contemporary Cuban artist working in sculpture and mixed-media with nautically themed artwork, inspired from La Isla de La Juventud where he grew up.

A graduate from La Escuela Nacional de Arte, he created the **Museo Orgánico Romerillo** (MOR) in 2014, in his old hood right near the arts school. He was inspired to lift up this marginal neighborhood by turning it into a museum without walls by placing art installations in the streets for everyone to see, and striving to help budding artists take flight. [Calle 120, corner Avenida 9; +537 208 0965; open Monday to Saturday, but call for appointment if you want to meet KCHO]

KCHO has been working in Pinar del Río to help schools and spaces destroyed by Hurricane Ian in September 2022 to recover. And to continue inspiring neighborhoods, as he does so well, he converted an abandoned rice-drying plant in the eastern province into a museum also called MOR, serving as a cultural hub and exhibiting his own works, part of his personal collection and other Cuban artists.

257 A

with a rooftop restaurant bar, Yarini, owned by his son Adán, one of his four children.

After many years of serving as president of the Gibara International Film Festival, Perrugoría is now president and founder of Isla Verde Festival Internacional de Cine y Medio Ambiente del Caribe (Isla Verde International Caribbean Film and Environmental Festival) inaugurated in 2023 in Cuba's Isla de La Juventud (Island of Youth).

The photo of Pichi shown here was taken in Gibara, where he told me about his favorite places in hometown Havana: Galería Taller Gorría and Yarini (Reason #56); the restaurant La Guarida (Reason #124), and the bar O'Reilly 304 (Reason #105).

257 B

Pichi Keen

257 **Jorge Perugorría** (A), known to Cubans as Pichi, is the country's most internationally recognized actor. After starting out in theater, Perugorría switched to the big screen following his breakout performance in the Oscar-nominated 1993 film *Fresa y Chocolate (Strawberry and Chocolate)*, in which he played the protagonist Diego, a happy-go-lucky gay man who meets David, a straight university student played by Vladimir Cruz. Since then he has acted in more than 50 films, including Steven Soderbergh's *Che*, which starred Benicio del Toro.

Perugorría is also a contemporary artist. He opened the **Galería Taller Gorría** (B) (Reason #56), an art gallery in Old Havana

257 B

Romantic Ruins: Cuba's Abandoned Art Schools

258 One day in 1961, Che Guevara and Fidel Castro golfed at the swankiest country club in Havana—in military fatigues and combat boots—to play what they considered a bourgeois pastime. The course was practically empty as most of the elite members of the club had fled Cuba, leaving the revolutionaries on their own to putt and ponder about the future of the country with a few of their favorite photographers in tow.

It was then and there that they decided to take over the grounds and build a tuition-free national arts school to educate Cubans and the world's underprivileged in ballet, music, art, drama and modern dance.

The plans were grandiose, and three architects (Ricardo Porro, Roberto Gottardi and Vittorio Garatti) were hired to build a structure for each of the five disciplines from one design concept: a series of Catalan vaults (domes made of layered tiles) constructed from locally made brick and terra-cotta tiles.

The design was revolutionary, never before seen in architecture. But the project was never fully completed (for economic, ideological and political reasons) and several of the structures, including the ballet pavilion photographed here, fell into various states of disrepair.

In 2003, the site was added to the UNESCO World Heritage Tentative List in the Cultural category as one of the most important Cuban architectural structures with outstanding universal value to the world.

The **Instituto Superior de Arte (ISA)** (National School of Arts), housed on-site in the completed buildings, is generally considered to be one of the most outstanding examples of the modernist movement in Cuba. No other country in the world has a school like this!

It is not possible to visit this fascinating historical compound without a permit, but you can take a peek at the abandoned buildings—some of which have been partially consumed by an ever-encroaching jungle—and marvel at the ingenuity of these architectural masters and their amazing creations. [Calle 120, btw Avenida 9 and Calle 23]

Pork Excellence

259 If you like traditional spit-roasted pork, then you should head to **El Palenque**, a sprawling restaurant complex that specializes in traditional Cuban cuisine.

A local favorite for years, this huge eatery is ideal for large groups and has their own bakery, artisanal Italian ice cream parlor, grocery store and liquor shop where you can buy wine to drink at your table. They also have a takeout menu comprising suckling pork, black beans, rice, vegetables, ice cream and cold local beer. [Calle 17, btw Calle 174 and 180]

Modern Architecture on the Beach

260 Designed in 1953 by Max Borges Jr., the architect of Cabaret Tropicana fame (Reason #219), **Club Náutico** is a landmark with its emblematic central pavilion overlooking the sea.

It was a posh private club before the revolution, after which it became a hangout for civil servants.

The main building is a beautiful expression of the Modern architectural movement in Cuba with its massive multilayered concrete arches designed to let light shine through optimally. The wave-like structure blends into its surrounding seafront, making it a great backdrop for photographs. [Calle 152, corner Avenida 3]

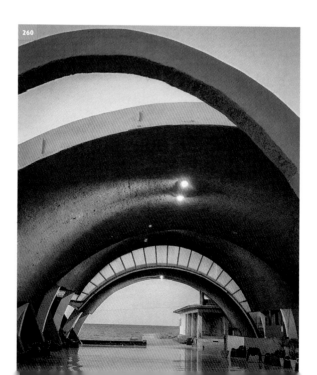

Walk in da Hood

261 Visit Buenavista, where you can see incredible larger-than-life photorealist painted murals of children's faces by **Maisel López**, whose work I adore. Daily life unfolds here in a simple and beautiful way and every corner tells a story waiting to be explored. Last time I biked through this vibrant community I paused to witness a 1950s vintage car stopping to let a chicken and her chicks cross the road.

One of Cuba's Most Versatile Musicians

262 Child prodigy **Alain Pérez** was born in the Cuban town of Trinidad in 1977 and started performing at the age of eight. Because of his inherent talent, the family moved to Cienfuegos so that Alain could sing in a children's band. He took singing, classical guitar and piano lessons, and later moved to Havana where he learned to play bass at the ENA (Escuela Nacional de Arte); he would become one of the best bass players in the world.

Alain was discovered by the eminent Cuban pianist and composer Chucho Valdéz, who later invited him to form part of his group Irakere. His first big gig was with famous Cuban musician Isaac Delgado, followed by an illustrious career playing with Celia Cruz, Los Van Van (Alain was the first person to stand in after the death of Juan Formell) and Paco de Lucía.

Considered one of Havana's most prolific bassists, composers and musical arrangers, Alain continues to rock the music scene with his solo albums, his spirited live perfomances and his boundless positive energy.

Two of his favorite spots in Havana are: El Malecón (Reason #128) and Paseo del Prado (Reason #116).

263

Urban Beach Club

263 In the 1950s, beach clubs lined the coast of Miramar and the Havana Biltmore Yacht and Country Club was one of the most spectacular. It even had a golf course and a baseball diamond. Now it is called **Club Havana**, and it still has the pomp. The gated entrance leads to a grand 1920s mansion that opens onto a beautiful quiet beach with chaises longues, umbrellas and a tiki-like bar. Right beside it is a huge pool with bar service.

There is also a restaurant, café, cigar lounge, gym, tennis courts and even a cancha court (Reason #240). The complex is also home to a number of diplomats and members of the business community, who live on the grounds.

For a fee, you can have access to this swanky private beach club for a day. It's a great place to take the kids. [Avenida 5, corner 188; +537 275 0100]

Om Santy, Santy, Fish, Fish, Fish

264 **Santy Pescador** might be a bit of a schlep, but it is certainly worth it. Set along the river bank in the peaceful fishing village of Jaimanitas, this prized spot serves up the best sushi in town, not to mention top-notch tuna tataki, ceviche and sashimi.

Named after Santy, a beloved departed fisherman, the restaurant that was his simple family home is now run by his four sons. There is no menu and everything depends on the catch of the day brought in their fishing boat, which is usually moored alongside the restaurant's wooden terrace. Check out the artworks by celebrated Cuban artists, including KCHO (Reason #256) and Roberto Fabelo, whose caricature of Santy is on display.

Anthony Bourdain made a stop here during his *Parts Unknown* Havana episode. [Calle 240A #3C23, corner Avenida 3 C; +535 886 7389]

Marlin Fishing and Modernist Homes

265

Marina Hemingway (A) is Cuba's primary marina where 400 vessels can dock, where the annual Ernest Hemingway Fishing Tournament takes place, a tradition that goes back to 1950, and the place to book a yacht for a unique day on the water. One of my absolute favorite things to do is sail away for a half day to fish, snorkel, and revel in the rare view of Havana from the sea. Call captain Alejandro Cordero [+535 283 7024] for a ride all the way to El Morro (Reason # 280). Don't forget your passport. The meeting point is right beside Papa's restaurant, a great place to grab a bite afterward.

At the western end of the marina is a remote island, **Villa Paraíso** (B), that comprises about 15 fascinating modernist houses designed by renowned Cuban architect Nicolás Arroyo and built in the early 1950s. [Calle 248, corner Avenida 5]

Just past the marina entrance is the incredible **Marea** (C), a seaside tapas and cocktail bar with beach chairs and swimming dock right on the crystal-clear lagoon. (Avenida 5 #25804, btw 258 and 260; +537 271 1192)

265 A

265 C

264

The Happiest Neighborhood

266

Called the Antoni Gaudí of Cuba and the Picasso of the Caribbean, **José Rodríguez Fuster** has transformed his poor neighborhood in Jaimanitas into a whimsical wonderland built of colorful tiles. When I saw it for the first time, I was propelled into a fairy tale. **Fusterlandia** is definitely something to behold.

A sculptor, painter and ceramic artist, the unbelievable Fuster is a national icon. With influences like Cuban artists Eduardo Abela and Carlos Enríquez as well as Picasso, Brancusi, and of course Gaudí, his dream was to live amid art and he made that happen by decorating his home inside and out with multicolored ceramics reminiscent of Parque Güell in Barcelona.

Since 1994, more than 100 neighbors have let him (free of charge) transform their homes into equivalent masterpieces. What were once small wooden houses with chicken coops are now works of art covered with vivid mosaics that also adorn gates, benches, stairs, rooftops—basically every inch of surface for blocks around Fuster's studio home.

Go for an enchanting walk through the hood and make sure to stop into Fuster's fabulous studio where you can also buy his original artwork. Try to find the Unicorn Park! [Avenida 3A, btw Calle 222 and 226; Jaimanitas]

NUEVO VEDADO — ARROYO NARANJO — SAN MIGUEL DEL PADRÓN — CERRO

Nuevo Vedado, the extension of Vedado, is a quiet residential neighborhood with high-end 1950s real estate and the emblematic Acapulco Theatre. Within San Miguel del Padrón, San Francisco de Paula, where you find Ernest Hemingway's estate Finca Vigía, is a suburban area with small farms and mansions. Cerro is the continuation of Centro Habana, where the bourgeois class moved to little farms in the early to mid-1800s. Here you will find Estadio Latinoamericano, Havana's baseball mecca and home of the Industriales team. Arroyo Naranjo is one of the lungs of the city with Parque Lenin and the Zoológico Nacional.

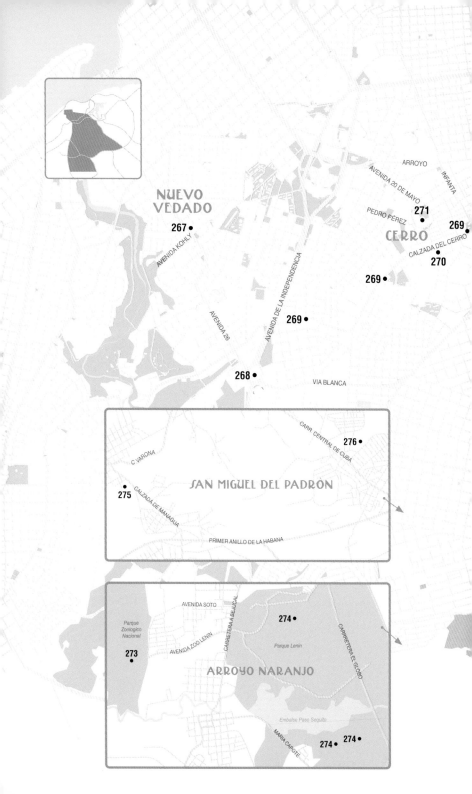

First-Run Films in Art Deco Ambiance

267 A landmark of pre-revolutionary architecture, **Cine Acapulco** opened in 1958 and was the last luxury movie theater to be built in the city. With its iconic marquee and modern-style detailing, it still flaunts the same ticket price of that bygone era, making it a theater that has remained accessible to all.

If you want an authentic Havana cinematic experience, head to this stylish venue and don't miss the magnificent timeless wall-length lobby mirror.

The theater is one of the official venues of the Havana International Film Festival; check it out if you are lucky enough to visit the city in December. [Calle 26 #3500, btw Calle 35 and 37]

Poking Fun

268 At one key intersection of the city near *Ciudad Deportiva* is a fountain called "La Fuente Luminosa" built in 1945 by architect-engineer José San Martín, the cousin of then-President Ramón Grau San Martín.

The central pillar of the fontain is in the form of upside-down cups, decreasing in size from the bottom up; each cup is illuminated in different colors from night until morning. The monument has entered into Cuban folklore because it was commissioned by Paulina Alcina, sister-in-law of the president. Alcina was the Republic's de facto first lady, as she was a widow and the president was single.

At the time, the locals concurred that the fountain was an extravagant expense and pompous undertaking. So, to mock the powers that be, they gave it the moniker **El Bidet de Paulina** (Paulina's Bidet).

Otherworldly Road

269 My favorite street in Havana is undoubtedly the dramatic and curvy **Calzada del Cerro** that became a stretch of palaces and summer residences for the elite in the 1800s as the population grew beyond the old city wall (Reason #54). This undulating three kilometer (nearly two miles) colonnaded road was one of the inspirational marvels of urbanism that fascinated novelist Alejo Carpentier (Reason #98), whose *The City of Columns* was a love letter to Havana. [From Infanta to Avenida de La Independencia].

An Art Hero of Our Time

270 "Everything I see runs the risk of being converted into a work of art," says internationally acclaimed visual artist **Esterio Segura,** born in Santiago de Cuba and "discovered" at his first solo show in Havana at just 21 years old, when he was asked to create sculptures for the landmark film *Fresa y Chocolate*. He graduated from Instituto Superior de Arte (Reason #258) two years later, in 1994.

He transforms cars, hearts, bottles and polar bears into flying objects with thought-provoking undertones. "We are all mentally flying to find freedom through the wings of our minds." At the 2017 Venice Biennale, his winged *Hybrid of a Chrysler Car* was the emblematic work on display in front of the Cuban pavilion.

Seamlessly incorporating limitless mediums, he pushes the boundaries of creativity and permissibility. "Everything I reflect on is in my work: I want to share

what I think. I want to say things that people are afraid to say." *Goodbye My Love*, his most iconic and loved series, is an installation of red fiberglass airplanes with a heart-shaped fuselage exhibited around the world, including Times Square in NYC, and in permanent installations at La Kunsthalle HGN, Germany, and Tampa International Airport by winning over 650 competitors.

"It's about the importance of immigration and the beauty of travel. Moving around is like getting a lecture about the world, you learn things and make a special connection with your surroundings." Always pointing skyward, it invites viewers to embrace the cycle of comings and goings with a sense of optimism and anticipation.

[To book an appointment at his eclectic studio, where works can be bought: WhatsApp +34 678 279 431; Calzada del Cerro 1313, corner Carvajal]

Take Me Out to the Ball Game

271 For many visitors, catching a baseball game in Cuba is as important as learning to dance salsa or smoking a cigar. If you like baseball, as I do, you won't want to miss this exhilarating experience.

The place to watch Cuba's national sport in Havana is **Estadio Latinoamericano**, home stadium to the local heroes, the Industriales, one of 16 national league teams representing major cities across Cuba.

Cuban fans are unbelievably vocal in their support (or disdain)—quite possibly the loudest and most passionate spectators of any live sporting event. As an outsider, don't make the colossal mistake of rooting for the visiting team. Otherwise, up to 55,000 Industriales fans may soon be glaring at you disapprovingly.

Games are normally played between November and April, though some international games take place during the off months as well. Tickets, available for tourists on-site from a small window around the back, are substantially pricey compared to what locals pay—but nonetheless a bargain by North American standards. In exchange for the price mark-up, tourists sit near first base and the home team's dugout.

The quality of the baseball is exceptional, though many of the best players have found their way into more lucrative leagues abroad, to the dismay of those who stayed. [Zequeira 312, Arroyo Naranjo]

The Man Who Loves Havana

272 Cuba's most famous writer, **Leonardo Padura**, lives on the outskirts of Havana in a simple town called Mantilla. There is a name on the entrance of his modest two-story house in which he was born in 1954: Villa Alicia, named after his 95-year-old mother. Leonardo and his wife Lucía live upstairs. "Although I can afford to move elsewhere, I am staying here with my parents. I can't move them. They are like two old trees. If you plant them in another location, they will die. I belong here."

Dressed in his Team Cuba baseball shirt, he made me coffee in his kitchen with his stovetop *cafetera*. "This is my special blend." A mixture of Juan Valdéz red with the black to smooth out the acidity.

We both agree that Havana is the city that most looks you in the eyes. "We have a gregarious nature and are very direct. The look is sensual and sexual. All men look at women's behinds and Cuban men love voluminous bottoms."

Why do you like baseball so much? "Because I am Cuban. I played next to my house when I was four or five years old. My father really liked the sport. The Industriales (Reason #271) has been my team for the past 50 years. I love them and want to kill them. Orlando Hernández, aka El Duque, left to play for the New York Yankees. It was a huge loss for us, but we know he wanted a better professional life for himself. We have to understand that."

What is the current situation in the country? "There are many serious problems in Cuba. The people are not happy with the status quo, and they are looking for solutions. Emigration is one of them. The majority of youth want to leave. We are losing our quality baseball players. We are in a state of crisis that has been going on since the 1990s. The FAC (Reason #207), for example, is full of people—lots of tourists, but lots of Cubans go there as well. When it opened in 2014, two to three drinks cost half the monthly salary of a doctor. This is one of the big mysteries about Cuba."

Is Havana safe? "I feel safe here; it is not a violent city. Yes, there is corruption and delinquency, but someone being held at knifepoint is very rare."

Do you have children? "I never had children, but would have loved to."

Where do you write? "I always write in my house."

Are your books sold in Cuba? "I am not censured, but not visible. I am not the one who is negatively affected, because I can promote abroad; it is Cuban culture that is losing the most. My book, *El Hombre que Amaba los Perros* (*The Man Who Loved Dogs*), which is about the failure of utopian socialism, told through the death of Leon Trotsky, has only recently been distributed on the island."

What is the role of a critical thinker in Cuba? "To create a critical consciousness, which isn't visible in the Cuban context. It is important to express yourself and speak about reality as you see it."

How do you see Havana in 20 years?
"I don't want it to turn into an amusement park for the United States. It could be modeled after Barcelona, which is attractive to tourists, but not made for tourists. The city is becoming a showcase for foreigners driving around in vintage convertible cars. The Havana of the future needs to be balanced in what it offers tourists and *habaneros*—it must be kind to the people who live here."

What do you want to do in the future? "If they don't kick me out, I want to stay. I am out of the country for three to four months a year to promote my books, but I always come back. I have a strong feeling of belonging to my city. Also, Cubans believe in nationalism, not communism. They believe in redistributing wealth to the poor."

What are your favorite places in Havana? The Estadio Latinoamericano (Reason #271). "I am always drawn there."

El Malecón (Reason #128). "It is a place with a soul. I always wanted to live by the sea, and Mario Conde, the protagonist in my detective novels, dreams of living by the sea."

Hemingway's Finca Vigía (Reason #276). "I used to make pilgrimages to his house, but now I only go there with visiting friends. My alter ego, Mario Conde, is a means to expressing how I feel about Hemingway.

"I can't say which restaurant is my favorite because I haven't been to them all, but I like Santy Pescador (Reason #264).

"It is not luxurious, and that is why I like it."

An International Success

Leonardo Padura is one of the island's most prolific writers—and definitely its most celebrated. He collected Cuba's top literature prize, *El Premio Nacional de Literatura de Cuba* (2012) and the Spanish *Premio Príncipe de Asturias de las Letras* (2015), the most prestigious prize granted for Spanish-language literature.

Padura's novel *The Man Who Loved Dogs* has been translated into a dozen languages and his detective series "The Havana Quartet" has been adapted into a screenplay by Padura and his wife Lucía. Watch the four-episode TV series *Four Seasons in Havana*. It stars Cuban actor Jorge Perugorría (Reason #257).

Lions and Tigers and Bears Oh My!

273 Located in the southern suburbs of Havana, to the south, **Parque Zoológico Nacional** (Havana National Zoo) is home to animals from around the world, some of which arrived in Cuba under the most interesting circumstances.

A rare condor was a gift to Fidel Castro from then Chilean President Salvador Allende. Many of the heftier animals were gifts from African leaders as a "thank you" for Castro's medical and military aid on the African continent. In 2012, the Namibian government donated nearly 150 animals to the zoo, including antelopes, vultures, hyenas, lions, leopards, cheetahs and porcupines in what was known as "Operation Noah's Ark."

To get around the zoo you ride a 30-year-old Girón-brand bus that simulates a safari around the animals' habitats. After the ride, you are dropped off at a recreational area with food stands where you can rent mini-scooters and buggies for children to whiz around the grounds. [Carretera Capdevilla, km. 3.5]

"Cuso," to get a peek inside the little building right next to the Sanchez monument to view unique revolutionary photos among the sleek modern 1950s furnishings. The park is also the locale for Havana's classic *Rodeo Nacional*.

There is also an amusement park (refurbished in 2009) with a Ferris wheel and roller coasters, horse rides, little boats to sail on the artificial lake and a very cool old steam train, among other attractions.

Right nearby are the National Zoo (Reason #273) and the Botanical Gardens with its picturesque Japanese gardens—a great place for a picnic. [Carretera 281]

Back to the U.S.S.R.

274 **Parque Lenin** is an enormous park and recreational area in the south of Havana that is double the size of Central Park in New York City. It contains a giant surreal bust of Vladimir Ilyich Lenin, carved in 1984 by Russian sculptor Lev Kerbel, that is one among the dwindling effigies of the revolutionary leader throughout the world.

There is also a monument to Celia Sánchez, Fidel Castro's comrade-in-arms who commissioned the park, in a beautiful leafy garden just around the corner from Lenin. Ask the park attendant, nicknamed

From Farm to Table with Fine Wines

275

With its arched Spanish patio overlooking its huge organic farm in the back, **Il Divino** is an epicurean marvel.

The menu is filled with irresistible BBQ options and the best paella that I've had in the city. One of my favorite parts of the experience was speaking with their pro sommelier and getting a tour of the red brick wine cellar decorated with unusual antiques and an imposing wooden tasting table resting on two huge wine barrels.

Il Divino is not just a restaurant: the staff is also involved in a lot of community projects, including providing lunches for the elderly in a beautiful cottage reserved exclusively for them in the middle of the farm.

This is a great place to take the kids because they can play in the huge yard and have delicious coconut-chocolate ice cream for dessert. [Calle Raquel 50, btw Esperanza and Lindero; +535 478 7433]

Hemingway's Havana Home: Finca Vigía

276

Located in San Francisco de Paula, about a 20-minute cab ride from Old Havana, **Finca Vigía** was Hemingway's home from 1939 to 1960.

The property went through such a thorough restoration job that you could almost expect Hemingway to saunter into the living room at any given moment with a glass of rum in one hand and a giant cat snuggled under his arm.

Talk to one of the museum guides walking around the premises; they are so knowledgeable on all things Hemingway that they appear to know more about him than he knew about himself!

While you are not allowed to enter the house itself, you can view all the rooms by circling around the open windows and cordoned-off doors. Stuffed trophy heads are hung on the walls throughout the house; books line every wall of the study. On Hemingway's bathroom wall are pencil marks of his weight beside an old scale as well as an embalmed frog. Hemingway's Underwood typewriter is displayed and propped up on a bookcase, where he used to stand and write because of chronic back pain.

Climb up the steps of the "tower" to see Havana's Capitolio building in the distance. The property gardens include an animal graveyard, where various pets were laid to rest over the years, and the dry-docked *Pilar*, Hemingway's beloved fishing boat.

You do not need to be a Hemingway fan to enjoy this historic jewel, but you may well become one after you visit! [Finca Vigía, San Francisco de Paula]

CASABLANCA — REGLA — COJÍMAR

Casablanca is a rocky hill across the bay from Old Havana where you will find the monumental Morro Castle, *El Cristo*, and the largest fortress in Latin America. From here you have the best view of the historic center. Regla is a fishing village, an industrial port and a mecca for Santería practitioners. This quaint suburb is hilly, filled with old wooden houses and hardly a car to be seen. It has a relaxed and rustic vibe. Cojímar is a quiet fishing village with charming seafood restaurants: it was the location chosen by Ernest Hemingway to dock his fishing boat *Pilar* and was the inspiration for the village in *The Old Man and the Sea*.

Hershey →

CARRETER...

COJIMAR

CASABLANCA

REGLA

287B
C

COJIMAR

MALECÓN

CALLE 1ra F

RIO

K

L

J

G

286

3E

5TA

287A

VIA MONUMENTAL

CASABLANCA

277

80

AVENIDA 1RA

LOS ALMENDROS

CARRETERA DEL ASILO

CARRETERA CASABLANCA

279

MALECÓN

AVENIDA DEL PUERTO

278

277

CENTRAL

281A

281B

LA PIEDRA

282

MARTÍ

BENITO ANIDO

CAMILO CIENFUEGOS

CÉSPEDES

PERDOMO

MACEO

RECREO

283

REGLA

AVENIDA ROTARIA

ANILLO DEL PUERTO

CALZADA DE REGLA

Sweet Adventure

277 The **Hershey Electric Railway** (also known as the Hershey Train) was originally built in 1917 for the Hershey Chocolate Company to transport workers from Havana to their sugar refinery 60 miles (100 kilometers) east of the city, and to send sugar to the port of Havana, through the station in Casablanca.

Milton S. Hershey, the American sugar baron, started building the model industrial town of Hershey in 1903 to serve as a housing development for his workers and gave the streets names like Cocoa and Chocolate. The town was later renamed Camilo Cienfuegos, after the revolutionary hero. The sign at the train station still says "Hershey."

The refinery closed in 2002, but the train continued to transport locals from town to town, running for a total of just over 100 years.

If you visit Casablanca by ferry, you can see the original departure point of the Hershey Train when you exit the *lanchita* (Reason #49).

Visit Christ Across the Bay

278 When you look across the Havana harbor toward Casablanca, you can't miss the 65-foot (20-meter) high white Carrara marble sculpture of Jesus Christ.

Created by Cuban sculptress Jilma Madera and weighing over 300 tons, it was brought to Cuba in 67 pieces from Italy, where it was carved; it was inaugurated on Christmas Eve, 1958.

As if by divine intervention, the humongous statue was hit by lightning three times before a lightning rod was installed to the right of the statue.

Seeing the statue up close is as awe-inspiring as the fantastic view of Havana across the bay. It is a great spot to contemplate, have a picnic or hang out into the evening when the local youth congregate.

As you get off the *lanchita* (Reason #49), follow the road uphill for about 10 minutes until you reach **El Cristo de La Habana**.

Sunset Feast, Wartime Relics and the Bang at Nine

279

When Havana was protected by a three-mile (five-kilometer) long stone wall (Reason #54) for nearly 200 years until it was demolished in 1863, there was a signal to let its inhabitants know that the city gates were about to close for the night. A single cannon was fired at precisely 9 p.m. from the **Fortaleza San Carlos de la Cabaña** on the other side of Havana's harbor.

Now you can see how it was done on the very same spot at the **Cañonazo de las nueve** ceremony reenactment. Performers, dressed in regal 18th-century military uniforms, march with torches and drums and fire a cannon into the night—followed by loud shrieks from the crowd.

The fortress itself was built to reinforce the city in 1763, the year after the British conquered Havana—which was returned to the Spanish, who were forced to cede the Florida peninsula, as stipulated in the Treaty of Paris that same year.

The fortress is more than 108,000 square feet (10,000 square meters) in size,

had at one time 140 cannons, and is now home to the **Museo de Fortificaciones y Armas** (Armament Museum)—a truly fascinating open-air collection of weaponry (mostly Soviet) from the days of the Cuban missile crisis, the **La Cabaña de Che Guevara** (Che Guevara Museum) and **Feria Internacional del Libro de La Habana,** the annual Havana Book Fair in February.

Go for a spellbinding sunset supper at **La Divina Pastora**, a state-run restaurant at the fortress that has the most privileged view of Old Havana and the bay. This gastronomic experience on the water's edge is unmatched as the sun says *"Adios!"* behind the iconic El Morro beacon (Reason #280).

Luminary Tower
and Tapas

280 The **Castillo de los Tres Reyes del Morro**, simply known as El Morro, has secured the gateway to Havana Bay since the late 16th century. Take a trip to Havana's ultimate emblem, visit its Museo Marítimo (Maritime Museum) and climb up its landmark lighthouse before heading down for refreshments at **3 Carabelas**, a collaboration between Jíbaro (Reason #11) and Sabor Café (Reason #51), specializing in crafted cocktails, Cuban tapas (cassava tortillas with *ropa vieja* or crab enchilada) and coffee.

Religions
in Sync

281 Enslaved by the Spanish, the Yoruba people of Western Africa brought varied religious customs with them to Cuba, including trance (to communicate with their ancestors and with deities), divination, animal sacrifice, sacred drumming and dance.

Spanish colonial authorities outlawed these practices and imposed Catholicism on the Yoruba. To preserve their traditions, the enslaved merged their customs with those of Catholicism, as a cover-up. They did this by syncretizing their *orishas* (deities) from the pantheon of Yoruba with Catholic saints that had similar traits. *Ochún*, the orisha of love, is matched with *La Virgen de la Caridad de Cobre* (Our Lady of Charity), the patron saint of Cuba; *Changó* with *Santa Bárbara*; *Babalúaye* with *San Lázaro*; and *Obatalá* with *La Virgen de La Merced* (Our Lady of Mercy) to name a few.

When Spanish colonial planters saw their enslaved people celebrating on saints' days they figured they were falling into line instead of actually performing rituals related to their orishas. The Afro-American religion

later became known as Santería (aka *La Regla de Ocha* and *La Regla de Ifá*).

The provinces of Regla and Guanabacoa are the epicenter of Santería, which has been practiced in Cuba for 500 years. During colonial times, enslaved people lived in these outlying areas, while the Spaniards resided safely inside Havana's fortified walls (Reason #54).

The **Iglesia de Nuestra Señora de Regla** (A) with its The **Templo de la Virgen de Regla** [Calle Santuario, btw Máximo Gómez and Litoral] is a place of worship for devotees of both religions: The virgin at the altar, *La Virgen de Regla*, is a Black Madonna, proclaimed patron saint of the Havana harbor in 1714. In the Santería faith she is linked to *Yemayá*, the ocean goddess, who is the mother of all orishas.

The most sacred day for *La Virgen de Regla/Yemayá* is September 7, when thousands of pilgrims from both faiths pack the streets of Regla to celebrate this saint's day. The Madonna is brought out for a procession through the streets (B) and traditional Yoruba ceremonies are performed.

You can't miss the church when you exit the Regla ferry. It's straight ahead and to your left.

And, just up the street from the church, and to your right, is the **Museo Municipal de Regla** (C), filled with Santería-related artifacts. [Calle Martí 158, btw Eduardo Facciolo and La Piedra]

Hip-Hop Over to Regla for the Peña

282 The third Sunday of every month, Regla is the site of an incredible outdoor **block party** called **Obsesión del Otro Lado** (Obsession from the Other Side) hosted by Cuban pioneer rappers Alexey "el tip este" Rodríguez and Magia López of the group Obsesión.

The venue is a large abandoned yard in between buildings where the crowd grooves to the most diverse musical acts.

It is so high energy and the crowd is inviting—come check it out and dance along! If you want to be in the lineup, contact Alexey in advance at alexeyeltipo@gmail.com. You can present whatever you want: all types of music, dance and any form of creative expression are welcomed. Be sure to arrive early on the day so that the DJ can prepare your beats.

The fun starts at 5 p.m., and continues until 8, 9 or 10. Bonus: It is free! [located right beside Máximo Gómez 106, btw Facciolo and La Piedra] or just follow the sound of music when you exit the *lanchita* (Reason #49).

The View from Regla

283 Go up the tip top of Regla to view Havana from a unique vantage point and don't miss the surreal bronze head of Vladimir Lenin created by Cuban sculptress Thelma Marin in 1984. It is set into the mountainside with 12 white figures below cheering on the Bolshevik leader.

This hill was named **Colina Lenin** (Lenin Hill) by the socialist mayor of Regla to honor Lenin shortly after his death in 1924. This spot was the site of many protests against corrupt Cuban governments in the decades that followed.

Insider Tour of Regla

284

Beatriz (Betty) Estevéz is a certified yoga instructor, Thai massage therapist, Ayurvedic medicine practitioner, artist, amateur photographer, former law student and my friend. What I didn't know is that she also gives full-fledged tours of Regla, her adopted hometown, so close but yet so far from Havana. "I want tourists to feel the magic, creativity and resilience of our town, through a real connection with its people and its history."

Betty took me on a small hike up La Loma del Chivo, revealing captivating vistas where I photographed her, then down past the Parque Martí—the central square—to 2KFé, a café serving tacos, to the church Iglesia de Nuestra Señora de Regla (Reason #281). On the way back, we stopped at the central *heladería*, an ice cream shop with a vintage neon sign restored by Project Por Amor (out of Los Angeles) in conjunction with Kadir López, an internationally acclaimed Cuban artist. Our last stop was a jam-packed clandestine bar that you could never guess existed from the outside, where they only serve beer, cola and ham and chorizo platters. Just walking through the streets of Regla, past the charming wooden homes, is a journey in itself. [Call Betty to book a tour in English or Spanish: +535 396 2531]

photographers, and a leading image-maker of the Castro regime; he was the author of some of the most striking shots of the era, including his iconic *Caballería* (The Cavalry) photo of bearded victorious revolutionaries in straw hats advancing on horseback, bearing Cuban flags.

Claudia's photography is more conceptual and abstract, as she explores and critiques societal tendencies; she defends women's rights, gay rights and fights against machismo and violent war-inspired video games. Her images are intended to make people reflect.

In 2010, Claudia graduated from the University of Havana in Social Communication and has been a professional photographer ever since. She was commissioned by the Gran Hotel Manzana Kempinski (Reason #86) to produce 105 architecturally-inspired photos that are on display in the rooms, suites, halls and lounges. In 2019, she inaugurated the Raúl Corrales Galería (Reason #114) in Old Havana.

Claudia's favorite places in Havana: the Malecón (Reason #128), Parque Almendares (Reason #213) and the Hotel Nacional (Reason #160).

[To purchase Claudia's works, or visit the gallery: ccorralmesa@gmail.com; +535 268 8684]

Like Father, Like Son, Like Granddaughter

285

Claudia Corrales, born in 1987, grew up in a multigenerational family of photographers in Cojímar. Her father Raúl Jr. is a photographer and her grandfather Raúl Corrales was one of the most renowned Cuban revolutionary

Hemingway is Alive in Cojímar

286 The seaside town of Cojímar was immortalized by Ernest Hemingway in his book *The Old Man and the Sea* as the tiny fishing village where the old man lived. This is the inlet where Hemingway docked his fishing boat, *Pilar*, and where he celebrated his daily catch with long hours at **La Terraza**, a fisherman-turned-tourist hangout known in his book as The Terrace.

La Terraza is on everyone's Hemingway tour as well as a stop at the village square just down the street, where a bronze bust of Hemingway—inside a neo-Greco columned gazebo—looks out toward the sea.

In the sun-drenched dining room at the rear of La Terraza, you can peruse the eclectic collection of black-and-white photographs—they feature the American author in various stages of angler glory—while also enjoying the view of the bay. Don't miss the shot of Gregory Fuentes, who was the inspiration for Santiago, the "old man" on whom the novel was based.

At the front entrance, a long mahogany bar, behind which vintage wooden beer fridges house the cool ones, greets the thirsty. [Martí Real 152, btw Montaña and Río]

Papa was Hemingway's nickname in Cuba. If you have white hair and a white beard, don't be surprised if locals smile and call you *Papa*!

Cojímar Restaurants

287 **Ajiaco Café** (A), which gets its name from a chicken and potato soup, differentiates itself with its fine touches on everything from their genuine homemade Cuban cuisine with a twist, to the way they make their mojitos with dark rum and honey instead of the usual white rum and sugar. And don't miss their chocolate cheesecake dessert, a rarity in Havana. [Calle Los Pinos 267, btw 5ta and 3E; +537 765 0514]

What a treat to discover **El Portal de Cojímar** (B) on the northern tip of this quaint and adorable fishing village. With the friendliest of staff serving ham and cheese plates, *tostones*, fresh fish atop yuca and *moros y cristianos* and sizzling pizza out of a brick oven, you'll have a whale of a time. [Calle Morro, corner K, Cojímar; +535 542 2269]

DAY TRIPS

Spend the day on fine white sandy beaches and swim in the aqua waters of Playas del Este and Varadero to the east of Havana. Go west to the province of Pinar del Río to find the best tobacco in the world. Visit one of many plantations where you can witness first-hand how a *puro* is made and see the oxen-plowed red fields and palm-covered tobacco-drying houses.

Behold the magnificent mogotes surrounding the ever-so-popular town of Viñales. And head to Cayo Jutías, the secluded seaside paradise, or Cayo Levisa, the romantic island getaway.

299

298A
CAYO LEVISA

294
LAS TERRAZAS

298B
CAYO JUTÍAS

296
SAN DIEGO
DE LOS BAÑOS

295 SORO

299
VIÑALES

PINAR DEL RIO
297A

SAN JUAN
Y MARTÍNEZ
●297B

Isla de

298A

Estrecho de la Florida

293

HABANA

TARARÁ

288 289

SANTA MARÍA
DEL MAR

291

290

277

HERSHEY

292

BACANUYAGUA

MATANZAS

300

VARADERO

Golfo de Batabanó

entud

Historied Beach Town and Sleek Retreat

288 For a quick jaunt to the beach, head to the gated resort of **Tarará**, only 12 miles (20 kilometers) east of Havana. To gain access, you will have to show your passport, fill out a pass, and pay a small fee—a small inconvenience for gaining access to a nice and quiet beach.

Tarará was built in the 1940s by an American developer with 400 modern-style residences, a church, a movie theater, a yacht club and a boardwalk; its beach was considered one of the most beautiful on the island.

Tarará served a variety of functions after the revolution, one of them being to house convalescing Chernobyl victims. But now it is partly destitute, with abandoned buildings that give it a post-apocalyptic feel. It is somewhat eerie to drive past the concrete carcasses, only to have an angelic white-sand beach appear.

For a more intimate experience, go to the tiny secret beach next to the marina with a resto-bar that can serve you beachside on Bali beds or lounge chairs. Bringing your own picnic is also an option, as is fishing or diving on-site.

For an experience beyond compare, stay in a stylishly-restored 1950s beach house featuring every option under the sun, including private catering, live performances by the island's exceptional musicians and DJs, and beachside bar service and treatments inside cozy cabanas. [stay@tribecaribecayohueso.com]

Beach Bliss Right Around the Corner

289 Twenty-five minutes east of Havana you will find one of the rare stretches of white sandy beaches untrammeled by commercialism in this globalized age.

Wild, bare and beautiful, **Playas del Este** extends for miles from the small resort of Bacuranao, past Tarará (Reason #288) and Santa María del Mar (where I usually go), all the way to the town of Guanabo. This serene beachscape, with its warm Caribbean water a shade of turquoise I didn't even know existed, is a treasure.

It's completely mindboggling how a portion of the stunning strip in **Santa María del Mar** is completely devoid of goods and services. Hardly a hotel, restaurant or a store in sight, just one long seaside picnic. DIY Cubans flock to the eastern edge of Santa María del Mar on weekends, armed with coolers full of grub, rum and cold Cristal or Bucanero beer.

Camaraderie and music are guaranteed but be warned: a toilet or food stand may be hard to find. If you are looking for services, try to camp out closer to the Hotel Tropicoco, which does brisk business with novice beachgoers.

For an LGTBQ+ hangout, head further east along the strip past Mi Cayito and before the Río Boca Ciega Estuary.

Grab a cab to get there (you can ask for a return trip) or take the beach bus from Parque Central in Havana.

Glamp it Up!

290

A half-hour east of Havana lies **Hacienda El Patrón**, a 22-acre tropical paradise surrounded by a forest of royal palms, where glamor exists in perfect harmony with nature. After the awe factor wears off, treat yourself to a signature cocktail or freshly squeezed juice from fruit grown right on their private farm, like mango, chirimoya, guava or *mamoncillo* (Spanish lime).

The culinary experience takes traditional Cuban cuisine to a new level, where everything is prepared with organic produce and meats from the on-site ranch. I had the best ever *crema de calabaza* (creamy pumpkin soup), made here with a purple beet swirl, and savory chicken baked to perfection in an outdoor brick oven.

Retreat to cozy yurt-like tents with queen-size beds, porcelain bathtubs and running water, book an outdoor massage in nature, glide on a kayak, relax in a hammock under the palms or take a nature hike. The visionary owner, Roberto Carlos Chamiso, is a young, dynamic and engaging host who embarked on this project in search of a tranquil haven in nature that he could call his own. Once created, he couldn't resist sharing it with guests, making this resort an idyllic destination for a rejuvenating daycation or overnight escape from the city. [Pueblo Arango, Camino de San Gabriel 200, Guanabacoa; +535 316 6594]

A Farm with a View

291

Twenty minutes outside Havana you can indulge in an over-the-top organic farm-to-table lunch while listening to live traditional Cuban music, with chickens running around at your feet, at **Finca Vista Hermosa**, owned by Raúl Relova and Misael Ponces. Go for an agricultural tour of the land, witness how *guarapo* (sugarcane juice) is made, watch buffalos bathe in the pond and ride on horseback to the top of the hill for a panoramic view of the countryside where the farm gets its name: *vista hermosa* means "beautiful view."

This 60-acre agroecological farm produces vegetables, milk (they donate milk to lactose-intolerant children in Havana hospitals), artisanal cheeses and meat according to the principles of social and environmental sustainability, with no chemical fertilizers used on the crops. The bulk of the land is used to grow feed for its cows, goats, buffalos and Creole pigs, thereby ensuring the nutritional value of their products. The manure is used for compost and the biogas cooks the food and cheeses. OK, TMI!! Call +535 463 4832 to reserve. [Camino La Esperanza S/N, Bacuranao, Guanabacoa]

Breathtaking View

292

Some recognize the **Puente de Bacunayagua** as one of Cuba's engineering marvels, while others view it as the place to enjoy the world's best piña colada.

The remarkable bridge is the highest in Cuba at 361 feet (110 meters); it spans the Yumuri Valley along Via Blanca highway and connects the provinces of Mayabeque and Matanzas.

On the west side of the bridge is **Mirador de Bacunayagua** (A)—an observation deck with souvenir stands, a restaurant and a patio bar that serves up one-of-a-kind all-natural piña coladas. These aren't just any piña coladas. They are made from freshly squeezed pineapple juice, coconut milk, coconut water, coconut flesh carved out before your very eyes and seven-year-old Havana Club rum, blended with crushed ice and served in a hollowed pineapple. If you want, ask the bartender to hand you the rum bottle so you can have your own personal pour. [Via Blanca, km. 82]

Sustainable, Transformative Farm

293

Fernando Funes Monzote is an agronomist with a PhD who brought his technical know-how to the Cuban countryside to undertake a groundbreaking project. He and his wife Claudia plunged head first into **Finca Marta**, named after Funes' mother, with a vision to transform Cuban farming by combining pre-industrial farming methods and modern technology. When they got started, the undulating land was full of rocks and invasive weeds; it was particularly infertile. That didn't stop them. They transformed the place without herbicides or pesticides and with diversified crops and minimal water usage. It took them seven months to dig a well, breaking layers of rock using only a crowbar. Since 2012, they have been an example for the whole country on how to transform land into an agroecological farm with just the sweat of their brow, and they now act as a hub working with a network of farms, cooperatives companies. Book a farm-to-table feast as a group and discover this impressive rural masterpiece. [fincamarta.com; +535 266 2159]

Don't Zip Past This Eco Village

294

Las Terrazas is an eco-community with a population of 1,000 in the Sierra del Rosario mountains, about a one-hour drive southwest of Havana. It started out as a reforestation project by Fidel Castro in 1968 that was led by architect and politician Osmany Cienfuegos, the older brother of revolutionary hero Camilo Cienfuegos. The aim was to recoup the land that was devastated by generations of coffee plantations. Tractors were used to clear and seed the mountains with millions of mahogany, cedar and citrus trees, creating terraces around Lago San Juan. Then a village was built with homes, schools and clinics, after which it became a burgeoning artist community.

Las Terrazas was declared a UNESCO Biosphere Reserve in 1985 and, after the collapse of the Soviet Union, it opened to tourists.

Hotel Moka (A) was built soon after: the two-story colonial-style building blends into the landscape with a 100-year-old tree literally growing through the floors.

There is a zip-line route through the village, hiking and bird-watching in the lush natural surroundings, and swimming in the waterfall pools of **Baños del San Juan** two miles (three kilometers) south of Hotel Moka. Don't miss **Casa Polo Montañez**, the lakeside house of the beloved Cuban singer that has been converted into a charming museum.

Serene Soroa

295

Soroa, a lush hilly nature reserve located 50 miles (85 kilometers) west of Havana, is named after Jean-Pierre Soroa, a 19th-century French coffee plantation owner.

One of his descendants, Ignacio Soroa, built a massive hillside orchid garden on the idyllic property, which he used as a personal retreat in the 1920s. After lying idle for some time, it was converted into a tourist spot after the revolution. The staff is incredibly friendly and proud to talk about the abundant and rare collection of orchids.

The region, with its heavy rainfall, makes for luxuriant scenery and the perfect backdrop for a bike ride or a hike up to see the nearby waterfalls.

Stay at La Pelegrina, a charming traditional wood cottage right in the heart of the valley. [Carrera central de Sosos, km. 7; +535 315 3169]

296A

Bygone Fantasyland

296

San Diego de los Baños, located 75 miles (120 kilometers) west of Havana, is famous for its hot springs that teem with sulfur and magnesium, known to cure skin disorders and soothe rheumatism.

The hot springs, discovered in the 17th century, have seen the likes of numerous Cuban personalities, including Cirilo Villaverde, the illustrious author of *Cecilia Valdéz*, and Independence leader Carlos Manuel de Céspedes.

The **Balneario San Diego de los Baños** (A), which is slightly past its prime, offers soaks in the healing warm waters, acupuncture treatments and massages. [Calle 23, corner 42]

Accommodations can be found next door at **Hotel Mirador** [Calle 40, btw 21 and 23]. Or, just stop in for a drink at its relaxing poolside bar and follow up with a hearty classic Cuban lunch at their *ranchón*.

Not to be missed: **Hacienda Cortina** is a fascinating place that once was the grand estate of Senator José Manuel Cortina. He created a whimsical playground during the 1920s and '30s with a fairy-tale mansion, Carrara marble sculptures and bronze lions hugging the hilly terrain, an artificial lake, ornamental Venetian bridges, Japanese garden and acres upon acres of tobacco, coffee and citrus trees.

Although Cortina's residence fell victim to the ravages of time, most of his other marvels have survived or are being restored—a process that began in 2014. Birders, be on the lookout for rare species.

A Pilgrimage to Cigar Mecca

297

Pinar del Río, Cuba's most western province, is the world's best tobacco-growing region with its robust red soil and abundant precipitation in the summer and cooler dry air during the winter tobacco season (November to March).

This is the place to go to see how tobacco is grown, harvested, dried and fermented—as well as the entire cigar-rolling process. The best-known plantation is **Robaina Farm** in the fertile Vuelta Abajo region. It was made famous by tobacco farmer Alejandro Robaina, who was a living legend, winning national prizes year after year for his quality crops. He had the distinction of being the only person after the revolution permitted to put his name on a cigar when the *Vegas Robaina* brand, which received accolades from across the globe, was created in 1997; [contact Ivan (plantation guide), +535 331 2222; Finca el Pinar Alejandro Robaina, Cuchillas de Barbacoa, San Luis.]

Masterful **Hector Luis Prieto** (A) also fully loaded with accolades, has a tobacco farmwhose tobacco farm is on the road between Pinar del Río and San Juan y Martínez. The farm gives plantation tours, cigar-rolling demonstrations and, of course, cigar tasting. Prieto also has accommodations: log cabins perched on a hill overlooking the river for those wishing to stay on the farm for a day or two. And a rustic lunch offering spit-roast pigs and chicken to be enjoyed on their spacious *ranchón* with a view, rebuilt after a hurricane in 2022.

To book tables or rooms call +535 264 9191. [Finca Quemado de Rubí, San Juan and Martínez]

Paradise Islands

298

About two hours by car west of Havana and a 30-minute ferry ride, a stunning island reveals itself to you, part state-run resort and part virgin beach. At **Cayo Levisa** (A) the sand is so fine you want to dig your feet into it the moment you arrive.

The resort was built in 1988 with a grand vision of creating a natural haven of peace and tranquility.

This is the perfect place to read a book, go snorkeling, kayak, learn to dance salsa, play beach volleyball or just kick back and watch the sun set from your villa. Walk along the beach to your right for 20 minutes through the mangroves and you will get to the best part—the deserted bit at the eastern edge of the island; it's like a dream come true!

When in Viñales (Reason #299), try to head out for the day to **Cayo Jutías** (B) with its long white sandy beach and crystal-clear water. Just 31 miles (50 kilometers) northwest, the trip to this beachside paradise is so worth it! Go for a walk through the mangroves, take a boat ride to the deserted island in the distance or just enjoy the serenity of this faraway place.

When you leave the beach, notice **Faro de Cayo Jutías**, a black-and-yellow skeletal lighthouse built by the United States in 1902. On its centennial anniversary, it was proclaimed a national monument. This unique beacon is still in use today.

Mogotes and More

299

If you head out from Havana to the town of Viñales early in the morning, you may see grass cutters with machetes in the median of the Autopista de Pinar del Río with low light from the west casting soft shadows as they work.

If you leave around lunchtime, stop along the way for a garden-fresh feast at **Finca Marta** (Reason #293) or at **Finca Tungasuk** [Autopista Pinar del Río, km. 17.3; +535 431 1698), dreamt up by Nicaraguan-Peruvian duo Annabelle and Alfredo for a four-course farm-to-fork epicurean experience.

Just before you arrive in Viñales, after about a two-hour drive, make a stop at **Hotel Los Jazmines** for the best view of Viñales Valley where you can grab a cool drink and contemplate the implausible formations of the *mogotes*, steep-sided hills that dot the valley floor. [Carretera de Viñales, km. 25]

Bars, restaurants and lunches on the farm: **Mogote Café**, **3J Bar de Tapas**, **El Olivo**, **Los Robertos**, **Cubar and Finca Agroecológica El Paraíso**.

You can't visit without eating at **El Cuajani** (A), located on a small farm at the foot of one of the hills. This sustainable gourmet garden-to-plate dining haven is brought to you by welcoming hosts Berta and José, who offer you exquisite organic food made from what they harvested that very day. [Carr. El Moncada, km. 2.2, Dos Hermanas; +535 882 8925] Other Eats: Mogote Café, 3J Bar de Tapas, El Olivo, Los Robertos, Cubar and Finca Agroecológica El Paraíso.

Stay at idyllic **Finca Villaverde**, a cozy traditional thatch-roofed countryside home for peace and harmony in the most picturesque setting, with meals direct from their permaculture farm [4 km. from village; +535 305 8300].

Places to Stay
· **Casa MogoteArt Viñales** [+535 473 4118]
· **Viñales Lodge and Cabaña Mia** [+535 892 4800]
· **El Balcon del Ermitaño** [+535 343 8592]
· **Cubao Campiña** [+535 813 5895]

Things to Do in Viñales: horseback riding, zip-lining, biking, hiking, and visiting a tobacco farm.

299A

Relaxation and Revelry

300

Ahhh, **Varadero**, the sought-after seaside haven, a tropical trifecta: powdery white-sand beaches, those turquoise waters and celestial sunsets just two hours east of Havana. Unwind on the shores or party along Avenida 1ra, the main drag in vibrant downtown Varadero.

Here are some highlights.

Josone Park. A wealthy, whimsical and passionate couple created a retreat for themselves in the 1940s and named it combining the first three letters of their names, José Iturrioz and Onelia Méndez (José is the grandnephew of Havana Club rum founder José Arechabala). This wonderland now comprises a swimming pool, restaurants, bars, two playgrounds, mini golf, a virtual reality room and a pond where you can rent circular electric pedalos from Bar Varadero 1920 and also get an all-natural piña colada.

For a great bite try **Varadero 60** and **Salsa Suárez**, two of the first and most savory *paladares*, **Nonna Tina** (Italian), or **Wacos** (international). For a taste of

Havana classics, visit the Varadero offshoots of **La Bodeguita del Medio**, **El Floridita**, and **El Aljibe**.

For open-air live music, **The Beatles** has excellent classic rock cover bands, and **Calle 62** is also bustling. Try **Casa de La Música** for Cuban rhythms. Take in dinner and a show, then dancing at the venerable 1950s **Cabaret Continental**, or late-night clubbing at **Havana Club**.

Varadero Boulevard is an enclave of shops, restaurants and bars: **Casa del Ron** sells a wide selection of rum and gives tastings under a huge portrait of the Cuban Rum Masters. Stock up on cigars at **Casa del Habano**. Grab a coffee or beans to go at **Casa del Café**. Find the hidden bar at **Sakura** where they named a cocktail after me. You can even see how guarapo is made at Trapichito.

Xanadu Mansion (A), built in 1927 by French American millionaire Irénée du Pont, is now a luxury hotel-restaurant and the 19th hole of the **Varadero Golf Club**. Stop in for a decadent lunch or dinner on their grand seaside veranda and zip into the top-floor **Bar Mirador** for a drink, or just to admire the eclectic architecture and panoramic view. [cubavaraderogolfclub.com]

Set in a 1940s mansion, **Mystique Casa Perla by Royalton** is an adults-only luxury getaway situated on an immaculate beach just steps from town. Top all-inclusive resorts are **Meliã International**, **Royalton Hicacos** and **Iberostar Selección**.

As you can see, Varadero beckons you to live its Cubanness, and with its perfect beaches, you've only just dipped your toes in. And as my father sagely conveyed to me, always take time to smell the roses!

Index

The Index numbers refer to the Reasons to Love Havana, unless otherwise marked.